Dedicated to the Men of the USS Trout (SS 202)

On Eternal Patrol

Crew of the USS *Trout* (SS 202)
Submarine Force Museum and Library

JEWELDEEN "DEEN" BROWN, RMCM (SS), USN RET.
EDITED BY STEPHEN LEAL JACKSON, PHD

DARK
IS THE
HARBOR

TALES OF THE U. S. SUBMARINE WAR
AGAINST JAPAN IN WORLD WAR II;
THE WAR PATROLS OF USS TROUT (SS 202)

outskirts
press

Outskirts Press, Inc.
http://www.outskirtspress.com

ISBN: 978-1-9772-7344-4

Outskirts Press and the "OP" logo are trademarks belonging to Outskirts Press, Inc.

PRINTED IN THE UNITED STATES OF AMERICA

TABLE OF CONTENTS

ACKNOWLEDGEMENTS

First and foremost, I extend my gratitude to Mr. Jeweldeen Brown. These are his stories that we worked on together over the years to get them into publishing form; my contribution was merely to edit and provide source documentation where necessary. They are unique in that they expand and explain many of the events generally described in the official war patrol reports. In them we hear the voice of one who was on the scene of major historical events and has the perspective of the enlisted man with differing perspectives and experiences than those of the officers or later researchers.

I also express my gratitude to Jessica Brown Hoadley, Mr. Brown's daughter. She gave me permission to embark on publishing these stories and generously allowed me access to her father's collection of photos and ephemera, many of which appear in this book. Without her support and encouragement this project would not have been possible.

Finally, my thanks go to Ms. Wendy Gulley, archivist of the United States Navy Submarine Force Museum who aided me in using the unique resource of the U. S. Navy Submarine Force Museum and Archives.

LIST OF ILLUSTRATIONS

LIST OF ABBREVIATIONS

AK	Auxiliary Ship
BB	Battleship
CL	Ship Cruiser
CO	Commanding Officer
DD	Destroyer
FM	Frequency Modulated (Sonar)
IJN	Imperial Japanese Navy
MM	Machinist's Mate
MMoM	Motor Machinist's Mate
NAVPERS	Naval Personnel Manual
PC	Patrol Craft
POW	Prisoner of War
PSI	Pounds per Square Inch
QLA	Navy FM Scanning Sonar
RM	Radioman
RMC	Chief Radioman
SFM	United States Navy Submarine Force Museum and Library Archives
SS	Ship - Submarine
SUBLANT	Commander, Submarine Forces – Atlantic Ocean
SUBPAC	Commander, Submarine Forces – Pacific Ocean
TDC	Torpedo Data Computer
TM	Torpedoman
USN	United States Navy
USS	United States Ship

FOREWORD

STEPHEN LEAL JACKSON, PHD

I ALWAYS CALLED him Mr. Brown. He introduced himself as Deen, short for Jeweldeen, but I could not bring myself to use his first name. He was willing to have me use the more casual form, but I could never do it. Whether it was his age, a vigorous 92 when we first met, his many courageous experiences, or just the gentlemanly nature he exhibited, he could only be Mr. Brown to me.

In 2007 I began work on the project that started as a master's thesis and would become my first book, *The Men*. To collect primary source information about the enlisted submariner's experience in World War II, I approached the local chapter of Submarine Veterans of World War II in Groton, CT; at that first meeting I requested that members who were willing to be interviewed fill out the form I provided. I was pleased to find that many of the men wanted to participate in my project, and Mr. Brown was one of these. Others who were not interested either were unwilling to discuss their war experiences or they had been interviewed so many times and the promised "end-product" either book, article, or paper, never materialized. I was determined to be different and to honor their generosity with a tangible result.

Mr. Brown was one of the first men I interviewed. He invited me to his home in Montville, CT where he lived with his wife Lois. Though difficult to find, theirs was a cozy home set in a lovely landscape of rolling hills, fruit trees, and a picturesque brook. Every time I visited, they were both so welcoming and the atmosphere there was so comfortable. I am grateful for the true hospitality they showed me. Mrs. Brown became very excited one day when I arrived in a new car. As we talked, I learned that she had been a bit of a car buff when younger and understood and appreciated the style and performance of automobiles. A visit to the Brown's house had the feeling of visiting family.

When I began interviewing submarine veterans, I hoped that I would find a story or two that might give a first-hand account of a significant historical event of the submarine naval battles in World War II; with Mr. Brown I dug for coal and hit gold. During our first interview at his home I was dumbfounded to hear him describe his first year in the submarine service. I must admit, I could not believe what I was hearing, but as that interview, and all that followed, bore out, Mr. Brown had been on-scene for many of the most impactful WWII Naval battles and events where American submarines played a part.

Mr. Brown began his service on submarines during the days immediately following the Japanese attack on Pearl Harbor. Like many men who ended up on submarines he began his service as a battleship sailor. While waiting in San Diego he was exposed to and developed an attraction to the submarine service. He left there to go to his first assignment in Pearl Harbor, Territory of Hawaii, on the USS *Nevada* (BB-36) in late November 1941. His naval transport entered the harbor mere days after the attack where his first views were of the *Nevada*, stricken by the Japanese attack, aground in shallow water with decks awash. Smoke, fires, and various rescue and recovery events were still underway. Into this scene of chaos and confusion came a young radioman from Missouri whose time in San Diego pointed him to submarines. This desire was fulfilled by a harried personnel officer and, after a time as relief crew, he was assigned to the USS *Trout* (SS-202).

Any interviewer would have been more than happy with discovering an eyewitness to the days after the attack on Pearl Harbor, but that was just the beginning. On Mr. Brown's first war patrol the *Trout* was one of two submarines to provide forward reconnaissance for the Dolittle Raid on Tokyo. The next patrol took him to the Battle of Midway and the subsequent war patrols were full of events, experiences, and impacts that were often headline news. While Mr. Brown was onboard the *Trout* also supported battles like Pilau and Peleliu, participated in special missions like insertion and removal of men and materials from occupied Philippines, and was able to capture several shipwrecked Japanese sailors. The *Trout* attacked a wide range of enemy vessels; from tiny sampans and diminutive submarines to aircraft carriers. She amassed a proud record of Japanese shipping either sunk or damaged. Mr. Brown was at school for her last mission, where she departed and remains on Eternal Patrol, but she went down swinging with two large cargo ships credited to her account during this patrol.

Mr. Brown devoted much of his time and energy to the Submarine Veterans of World War II, at one point serving as the Connecticut State Commander. He was instrumental in transitioning the organization from a national to a regional organization when the decreasing number of WWII submarine veterans made this a necessity. Even in this new, smaller organization the duties of organization and leadership became more and more onerous for the aging membership. Mr. Brown facilitated recruiting Associate Members, members like me who had not served during the war, into these leadership positions. That was how I became the Vice President and Newsletter Editor of the Submarine Veterans of World War II – Eastern Division. All of us entrusted with the legacy of these men were honored and humbled by their confidence.

I thought of him much like you would think of an elder relative; wise, strong, and deserving of respect. He called me on occasion his shipmate; I have rarely been so honored. At the very end of his life, he called for me to come to his hospital room and asked me to write his obituary because, "You know my navy life the best." A simple request that I was humbled and honored to accept. He survived our last meeting by only a few days and, as I stated in the obituary, "We will not see his like again." It was my privilege to work with him as a researcher, a member of the Submarine Veterans of World War II, a grateful friend, and a shipmate.

S. L. J., February 2024

CHAPTER 1

CONVERSATION WITH
THE WILLING WARRIOR

THIS CONVERSATION TOOK place between Jeweldeen Brown, RMCM (SS), USN (ret.) and Stephen Leal Jackson, PhD beginning on January 17, 2007, and on several subsequent occasions. There has been some minor editing for clarity but for the most part natural speech and vernacular has been preserved so that the reader can have a similar experience to sitting with us in Mr. Brown's living room. When necessary, notes have been added to expand or explain. The remainder is an unalloyed conversation with the humble warrior who was willing to serve his country, his boat, and his shipmates in a time of his country's greatest need.

Stephen Leal Jackson (Steve): Thank you so much for taking the time to talk with me today, Mr. Brown. As you know, I am trying to research the enlisted submarine sailors during World War II and why they all volunteered for this most dangerous assignment. I am concentrating on the enlisted man because, well, I was an enlisted submarine sailor myself in the 1970's and 1980's but also because most of what has been written has been from the officer and commanding officer point of view.

Jeweldeen Brown (Deen): That is very true.

Steve: So can we start with how you came to join the Navy?

Deen: Yes, of course. To start with back in, say about 1939, Hitler was rampaging through Europe. Everyone in this country, at least where I lived, was quite sure that we were going to get into the war. And the draft had started. And most of my buddies were being drafted into the Army. Well, I'd done a little bit of research, and I was impressed with the educational programs that the Navy offered. And the Army, almost none. I felt that I needed an education and that was a good way to get it. Times were real tough back then. It was just a few years after the very famous Depression Years, you know, in the '30's? So I told my dad I said well, I'm not going to take a chance on being drafted in the Army, I'm going to go to Kansas City and I'm going to volunteer to join the Navy, which I did.

Steve: Where were you living at the time?

Deen: I lived in a small town in Missouri. My address at the time was Rockville. I was born in another small town nearby called Shell City. And those small villages are about ninety miles straight south of Kansas City. Almost on the Kansas border and so a lot of business things such as joining the military, I had to go to Kansas City to do that. So I went to Kansas City and in March of 1941 I joined the Navy.

And I was immediately sent out to the Naval Training Center in San Diego. They kept me there on a work detail for a little while but then I protested and finally they put me into a Training Company which was Company #52. My company number was 4152, 41 being the year, of course. And I graduated from the boot camp and was assigned to the battleship USS *Nevada* (BB 36).

Navy Recruit
Jeweldeen Brown
Author's Collection

Graduation Photo for Recruit Training Company 4152
Author's Collection

Nevada was stationed at Pearl Harbor in the Pacific Fleet. Back then, Steve, all of the military, Army, Navy, Marines, and so forth, were building up very rapidly and the Navy especially. And there was a very acute shortage in the Navy, at the time, of several rates particularly technical rates like, well even Machinist's Mate, Electrician, Fire Controlman, Radioman: a very great shortage of them. And so I applied for radio school when I was in boot camp. Well, when I was assigned to the *Nevada* they sent me orders that said, you go to radio school first and then you report to the *Nevada*.

Steve: You were able to get the school you wanted.

Deen: Yes, I walked out of boot camp and walked right into radio school, it was that close. I graduated from that by, oh, along about

Radio Group II School 10-1941 San Diego
Author's Collection

October, September, or October, graduated from the radio school.

While I was there, I met some submarine people. They were off of the old "S" boats. There was a squadron of "S" boats in San Diego at the time and they were going to school; some of them were going to school there. And I was impressed with them because they all seemed to be a lot smarter than I was! They were breezing through the course that I was struggling to make a 3.5. I thought, my, those guys are okay maybe that would be a good outfit to get into; it was in the back of my mind, you know. And also while I was in the radio school there was an old, retired chief and he'd been recalled into the Navy. He was there on duty, and I would talk with him and he would encourage me to get into submarines. "Oh, that's good duty, you'll learn a lot, you'll get an education" he said, "that's the way to go."

Steve: I think that was good advice.

Deen: I agree, but, you know, so to go back a little bit, before the war, Steve, all sailors had to spend one year minimum in the surface Navy before you could even apply for submarine duty. That was a mandatory requirement. I had not met my one year yet, I was a little short of that, you know. So I figured, as soon as I get my year in I'll put in a request. Well, I graduated from the radio school, and I had to hang around San Diego for a month or so waiting for transportation to go to Pearl Harbor where the *Nevada* was. They stationed me out at what is now the submarine base at San Diego, they have the tender there and the nuclear boats berthed, but at that time that base was called a section base. And they had a fueling depot there for the submarines, so they moored there, the "S" boats did. And also, they operated from that base what they called a harbor patrol, small boats that patrol the harbor. And there was a radio station there and so forth, so they put me on duty there, awaiting transportation.

So I was there, I don't know, a month or six weeks or so, and it was a small base and there was really nothing hardly there.

Steve: Now can I ask you, the submariners that you met, did they ever take you down onto the boats, the boats were there in San Diego, the "S" boats?

Deen: Yes. For instance, there was no ship's service store, no geedunk stand, if you got hungry it was just too bad; if you didn't have something in your locker you went hungry. But I found out that the guys on the "S" boats had food all the time. And most of the time they ate very good, you know, so as soon as I found that out, I'd go down to the "S" boats, visit with those guys, and eat whatever they had to eat, and, yeah, so I spent quite a lot of time talking with them, you know and so forth.

Steve: Did you ever happen to go down on one and take a tour?

Deen: Oh yes. I was rather intrigued with the complexity, and I was somewhat awed that these guys could learn to operate that thing. Because going in there and looking around it's like walking into the cockpit of a 747 airplane and looking at the cockpit there. You know, instruments everywhere, all of that, of course, was mysterious to me. And so I was somewhat awed by that, and I thought, you know, gee, just to learn how to operate this thing would be an education in itself. I had some mechanical ability before that because my dad had operated a garage and a gas station, and I used to help him quite a bit. Well anyway, that's how I remember my impression of the "S" boats; and I knew I wanted to get into the submarine force.

Steve: Very fortunate that those "S" boats were there.

"S" Boats in San Diego; USS *S-42, S-43, S-44, 45, S-46, & S-47*
Public Domain Image: http://navsource.org/archives/08/
sboats/0815306.jpg [accessed 3/6/2024]

Deen: I truly was. Well, I finally got on a Navy ship and headed for Pearl. And while we were on the way for Pearl Harbor the Japanese bombed the place. And the only thing I knew at the time was, the only thing we'd heard was that they had sunk the battleships *Oklahoma* and *Utah*. And so, we arrived in Pearl Harbor which was a few days after the raid.

Steve: I can't imagine. What was that like?

Deen: Well, going into the harbor, the very first thing I could see, the very first ship I could see as you entered the harbor was, in fact, my ship, the *Nevada*. It was sitting there near the mouth of the harbor aground with decks awash, you know. I looked at that and I recognized it immediately because the superstructure was a bit unique, and I knew it was my ship. So I knew also that I had to find a new home, I wasn't going to go on that one.

Steve: No, I guess not!

Deen: So we docked in Pearl Harbor, and my ship was sunk and my first thought was, "Well, I have to find some of those *Nevada* officers." After all I had orders, you know, to the ship so I should seek

USS *Nevada* beached & burning after Pearl Harbor attack.
https://www.history.navy.mil/our-collections/photography/us-navy-ships/battleships/nevada-bb-36/80-G-19940.html [accessed 3/6/2024]

out the crew. I thought that certainly, there must be some of those officers, probably in some building or somewhere in Pearl Harbor. I'll find them and report aboard. Well, I searched for them for the better part of a day and nobody even heard of them, the place was chaotic anyway. My little problem was not a concern to those men with really big problems. Because, you know, there was still a whole lot of activity going on and the harbor was filled with oil and fires were still burning and divers were going down after bodies, and the place was really chaotic.

Steve: How long after the attack did you arrive in Pearl Harbor?

DARK IS THE HARBOR

Deen: If I remember right, I arrived in Pearl about nine or ten days after the attack. So anyway, I realized then that there was probably a window of opportunity for me to get into submarines even though I was not yet meeting all the criteria. So I made my way up to the receiving station, I don't know if the Navy has them anymore but they used to have personnel receiving stations. And whenever you went into an area, such as, like Pearl Harbor, if you had to wait on a ship or for some reason or problem that you couldn't go to your assigned station you'd go to a receiving station, it's kind of a holding station. I went to the receiving station and I reported there and showed the officer who was on duty my orders and he says, "Well, you're not going to the *Nevada!*" and I says "I know that sir, but where am I going?" Well, he looked like he hadn't had any sleep for a about a week, hadn't shaven and he was tired, and irritable, and everything you know. He rubbed his head and said, "Where would you like to go?" I said, "Well sir, I think I'll go to the submarine base." He looked at me, paused for a moment, then filled out a piece of paper and said, "Goodbye and good luck."

Steve: You solved his problem!

Deen: Yes, that one anyway. I solved his problem, and he helped me. So I went to Subase and got to the gate. Of course, Marines guarding there, sentries and all that and they wanted to know what I was doing there carrying the seabag. The receiving station was at Hickam Field; all the way out there. I had to walk all the way there from the Navy Base carrying my seabag clear to the Subase, maybe two miles. I got there and I told the Marines at the gate I wanted to report; I wanted to talk to the personnel officer. So he of course asked me what I was doing. I told him I said well, I'm looking for a duty station; I'm adrift. I said I want to see the personnel officer.

So he gets on the telephone and he makes a phone call. He sticks his head out of the shack and said, "What's you rate?" I said, "I'm a Radioman." I was a designated Radioman although my rate was Seaman First Class then. He said, "You stay right here, they'll be a jeep for you!" So I knew I was in.

Steve: They sent a jeep? Radiomen must have been in high demand.

Deen: They were. After the raid, communication was a high priority. Well, I got to the Subase and by that time it was like 7 o'clock, 6 or 7 o'clock in the evening. And I'd been running around all day there looking for those *Nevada* officers and I was hungry and I was tired. I got to the personnel office, and they said to me, said, "Don't bother unpacking your bag you go right directly to the Subase radio station because they want you." So I said, "Well sir, I haven't had anything to eat all day since breakfast, I'm awful hungry. Is there something up there to eat?" He said, "No, but we've got about five or six other guys that haven't eaten so we'll send all of you to the mess hall and they'll feed you." So they did that and after some chow I went to the radio station and that place, Steve, was a beehive of activity. And I went immediately on-watch there on a radio circuit. We were handling an awful lot of traffic to the United States. A lot of it was personnel information, trying to answer queries about sailors who had been there and were missing and so forth.

Steve: My ignorance here, but was that voice communication?

Deen: No, no. Morse code. We hardly ever used voice communication. All of it was Morse code. Anyway, I was on-watch there for, oh, probably till about 1 or 2 o'clock in the morning the first day. And finally, another Radioman showed up and relieved me. So I said to my supervisor, "Well, I guess I can go to the barracks now and unpack my bag and maybe get some sleep." He says, "No, you're not going to the barracks." I looked and him and said, "No?" He said "NO! You go outside, you'll get shot!" At that time, there were sentries all over the place there, National Guard and Army and sailors and Marines and everything; anticipating an invasion. Some of them were a little trigger-happy. And some of them were shooting first and asking questions later, you know. And so he told me, "Don't go out there; you're just apt to get shot." So I stayed there all night even though I didn't have anything to do except help out a little bit where I could. And so next morning, at daylight, then I went to the barracks and got my bag unpacked and so forth. That was my first introduction to the submarine Navy.

Steve: That is a long day!

Deen: It surely was. So I was there, based at the station, at the radio station at Pearl Harbor, Submarine Base and not only were we handling all the traffic for the submarine Navy, but for the other parts of the Navy as well, including Commander in Chief, Pacific Fleet. Their headquarters was just across the channel. I don't know where they're located now but they used to be just about straight across the harbor towards the shipyard there from where the Subase is. But anyway, we were handling radio traffic for them as well as the Subase and anybody else, I guess, that needed it. So, it was a busy, busy place. It was also at times alarming to me or disheartening because it was lists of deceased people we were very often transmitting. Sometimes I would see either one of my classmates or one of my bootcamp mates, people that I knew. It was a shock, of course, and that was saddening, but I had to do my job and keep going, you know.

Steve: Sir, I can't imagine what that was like for you.

Deen: Well, very sad, very sad. So I was there at the Subase for four weeks or so. They hadn't told me anything and I was wondering, "What are they going to do with me? Am I going to stay here, am I going to be transferred, or what?" So finally my curiosity got the better of me and I went to see the personnel officer told him, I said, "You know, I been here for four weeks and I'm just wondering if you had any plans for me, and if so, what are they? Am I going to stay here?" He said, no, you're not going to stay here. In fact, we're going to transfer you over to the USS *Pelias* (AS-14). You may have heard of the *Pelias*, it was a submarine tender.

Steve: Yes, I have heard of her, but I think she was decommissioned before I joined.[1]

Deen: Right. The Navy had about, by the time the war ended, they had about six submarine tenders that were, in fact, converted merchant marine merchant ships, freighters; they were big freighters, large ships. *Pelias* was one of those. We called her the "Banana Boat", a converted banana boat we thought, but it was a good ship. Anyway, they did transfer me to the *Pelias* and now I was in Submarine Squadron Six which was headquartered onboard the *Pelias*. And here I was, getting a little closer to the submarines all the time.

Steve: How long were you on the *Pelias*?

Deen: I stayed on the *Pelias* for, let's see I went on in January, and I stayed on there until March (1942). I volunteered for submarine duty. Even though I had been working around submarines for weeks you had to volunteer for sub-duty to get on the boats. The submarine force was all-volunteer.

Steve: It's that way to this day.

Deen: Exactly. I made third class when I was on the *Pelias*, third class Radioman, and they put me in a relief crew; the *Trout* was there along with other squadron boats. All the Squadron Six boats at that time, there at Pearl Harbor, were all brand new boats; the very latest boats that had been built were sent out there to form Squadron Six. And that was what we called the "T" boats, and the "G" boats. The "T" boats were *Tambor, Triton, Trout, Tuna, Tautog, Thresher.* The "G" boats *Gar, Grayling, Grampus, Grayback, Grenadier, Gudgeon.* While I was on the relief crew I worked on the *Tuna.*

Steve: It must have been good to work on and ultimately be assigned to a newer boat.

Deen: The *Tambor* class boats, which the *Trout* was one of them, structurally speaking they had a weakness. The weakness was that they had only one engine room and it was a very long compartment. I didn't even have a king frame. So, later, starting with the next class of boats, which was the *Gato* class, they put a bulkhead in the middle and had two engine rooms.

Steve: I was just going to ask, if that, would you say that was the major difference between *Tambor* and *Gato* classes?

Deen: Yes. And, of course, as the classes progressed, the quality and thickness of the steel improved, so their depth capability also increased.

Steve: I see.

Deen: *Tambor* class boats, their test depth, I think if I remember right, was something like 318 feet.[2] We used to take the boat to 400 feet routinely. It didn't bother it. It would go, you know. And we did that for a long time, you know, to get rid of, to get out of the way of the depth charge attacks.

Steve: That's knowing your equipment for sure. Okay, let's get back to Pearl Harbor. Now relief crews replaced the regular crews while in port after a war patrol, is that correct?

Deen: Yes. After a war patrol, the crew would get rest and recreation; it was sometimes almost a month but if the Navy needed you back out there, much shorter. But the relief crew would come on, stand watches, do repairs and overhauls, and get the boat ready to return to see while the crew rested a bit.

Steve: I see.

Deen: Sometimes we had a little chance to have a little recreation ourselves. Here's me, second from the right, on the beach in Honolulu. It was Waikiki, near the Royal Hawaiian which was being used a Submarine rest Camp.

Steve: Yes! Great photos.

Deen: Well, my first job, in fact, was to overhaul the electronic equipment onboard the *Tuna*. And my first boss was a young Lieutenant by the name of George L. Street, III. You undoubtedly have heard of him; he was one of the Medal of Honor recipients and he had command of the *Tirante* during World War II.

Steve: Absolutely! He received the Medal towards the end of the war, is that right?

Brown on Waikiki Beach 1942 (2nd from right)
Author's Collection

Waikiki Beach with Royal Hawaiian in the background
Author's Collection

Deen: Yes, In 1945. Well, he was my boss then, and a very fine fellow. And taught me a few things I might say. I did a little bit of work on the *Trout* as well; in fact, I helped load the *Trout* with ammunition because they were going on a special mission to the Philippines. The Philippines had not yet fallen to the Japanese but most of the military was marooned on the island of Corregidor, and *Trout* was going to take a load of ammunition in to them, because they needed it badly, which she did. I volunteered to, I tried to get onboard the *Trout*, but they had a full complement of Radiomen, so they really didn't have place for me. But the Exec told me, well, when we come back, if you're still in the relief crew I'll take you aboard because I'll have to transfer one of my Radiomen when I get back, so I'll have an opening for you.

Steve: I'm just trying to get what your motivation is here. You're in Pearl Harbor, you're contributing and working in your rate but you wanted to get on a boat that is going into harm's way?

Deen: Yes, exactly. I wanted to get on a submarine, I really, I wanted to get the experience, and I wanted to be a qualified submariner.

Steve: And the danger was...?

Deen: Not something I thought about. I was young and like most young people I was invincible! [we both laughed] So, anyway, when *Trout* got back from that particular patrol run sure enough, the Exec was as good as his word and he did transfer one of his Radiomen and he brought me aboard. I went aboard the *Trout* in March of 1942. The first thing I did when I went aboard the *Trout* was help them unload billions of dollars in gold and silver![3]

Steve: I've read about that!

Deen: Almost everybody has. The captain actually went ashore and the boat was light because they didn't have a load of torpedoes. In fact, the situation in the Philippines was so bad that they didn't have any torpedoes to give to them. So, they were very light and they needed ballast. The captain requested if they could use, you know, not going to overdo things, he requested sandbags. Well sandbags were precious since they expected a Japanese invasion! So, they told him, "You can't have sandbags but, you know, we've got this load of gold and silver, you can take that." That's the way it happened.

Steve: Solid gold and silver for ballast; isn't that something!

Deen: Not its intended purpose, but it worked just fine. So, at any rate, I helped them unload all that stuff; I have a few scraps of some paper I got off of packages of Philippine pesos, the wrappers you know. I have those in my scrapbook.

We unloaded all that gold, silver, and special important papers onboard the cruiser *Detroit*. And then the *Detroit* carried all that money back to San Francisco where it was kept for the Philippine government until after the war. *Trout* was very, very famous for that particular run and after that run General Douglas MacArthur awarded all

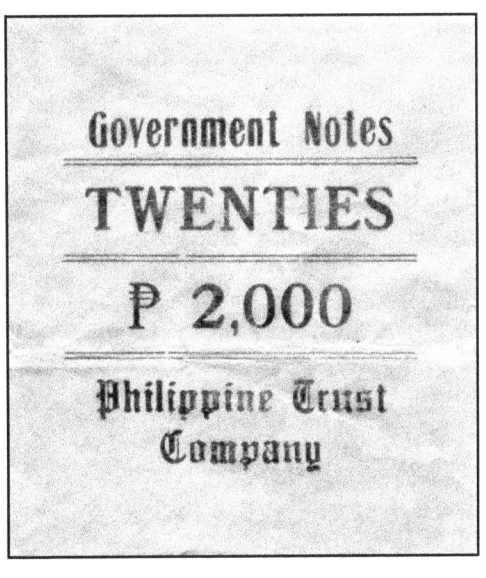

Government Notes

TWENTIES

₱ 2,000

Philippine Trust Company

Philippine Money Band
Author's Collection

Photo # NH 90389   USS Trout comes alongside USS Detroit, at Pearl Harbor, March 1942

USS *Trout* comes alongside
USS *Detroit* to unload gold.
*Submarine Force Museum
& Library Archives*

hands on the *Trout* except the captain, the Silver Star medal. From the mess cook right up to the Exec got the Silver Star medal. I don't think the high-ranking naval officers approved of the award but all hands on the *Trout* were awarded the Silver Star.

Steve: Amazing! The Silver Star!

Deen: I've read quite a bit of history written after the war and that act created a bit of consternation amongst the high-ranking naval officers. They did not look upon MacArthur awarding sailors as his prerogative, you know, and that caused some dissention between the Army and the Navy, and I guess finally MacArthur was told, you don't award our sailors medals. Even though, administratively though, the Navy in the southwest Pacific came under MacArthur's command. There was a little bit of a caveat there. Operationally the submarines came under the Navy's command but administratively they were under MacArthur. It was kind of a strange deal. Well, at any rate, all hands on there were awarded the Silver Star. I think it's the only ship in naval history where that's ever happened.

Steve: I guess I can see both sides of that argument.

Happy new *Trout* crew member Brown topside underway
Author's Collection

Deen: I can too. So that was my introduction to submarines. After getting on board there in March we sailed at the end of the month on the *Trout's* third war patrol, that would have been my first one. And our mission at that time was secret. We didn't have any idea what we were supposed to do or would be doing, but we were ordered to take a course for Japan. The captain could not open his orders until we were underway for forty-eight hours after a stop at Midway Island. We would stop at Midway and top off fuel. Forty-eight hours after that, according to his orders, he could open his orders then he could tell us what we were going to do. So that happened and we found out that we were part of Task Force 16 and we were to partici-pate in the Admiral Halsey / General Doolittle bombing raid on the Japanese homeland.

Steve: That was your first war patrol? That was one of the most famous naval actions of the war!

Deen: True, but I didn't know it at the time! Of course, that task force, being a carrier task force, had two carriers in it, the *Hornet* and the *Enterprise*. All told I think there were seventeen ships in the task force including the two submarines. Of course they were much faster than we were so naturally we had to proceed well ahead of them so they wouldn't run over us. We arrived off of Japan, we, I say, the other submarine was the *Thresher*; the first *Thresher*. We arrived off Japan several days before them but part of our mission at that time was to provide intelligence back to Admiral Halsey. Because that was a risky, risky operation. Traveling all the way across the Pacific Ocean, just like the Japanese did at Pearl Harbor, and getting to a few hundred miles off the coast of Japan without being detected, you know, and then challenged by the Japanese Navy, was really rolling the dice. They needed intelligence and the only types of ships that could provide them with intelligence at that time were the submarines. They couldn't do it by air. There was no other way.

Steve: Yes, of course.

Deen: *Thresher* was ordered to monitor the Japanese fleet in Tokyo Bay, so she took station at the entrance to Tokyo Bay. We were ordered to do the same thing off of Kobe, because those two bases were the largest naval bases for Japan. And if they had detected the task force we would have seen them coming out *en masse*, you know, a sortie. And if they had done that, it would have been obvious that they were heading out to challenge Admiral Halsey. So we laid right off of the entrance to, I think it's called Kii passage[4] which enters into the Sea of Japan, and then Kobe is a little farther on inside the Sea of Japan. We stayed there for several days, days and nights, watching for the Japanese fleet. Of course, they didn't show up.

Steve: Was that your only task on the mission?

Deen: We also had to send weather reports providing the weather was going to be inclement and would interfere with visual bombing. Those pilots would fly low altitude. They could not take the bombsight, because the bombsight was highly classified, and we didn't want to risk losing that bombsight and have the Japanese get that technology. They took the bombsight off, the so-called Norden bombsight, and they had to bomb by visual means, and we knew that, and they couldn't do that unless they had good visibility.[5] If the visibility was bad, we had to tell them, if it was okay, we didn't say anything. The reason being, we maintained radio silence as much as possible because we did not want to alert the Japanese that we were in the area. So when the weather turned out to be nice and clear, it was good, so we didn't have to transmit. The Japanese didn't come out, and we didn't have to transmit. So far, we were scoring ten for ten.

Steve: So you were only to transmit for bad weather or a Japanese sortie?

Deen: Correct. Well, the raid took place although it took place early. We were so far ahead of that task force, Steve, we were days ahead of them. We were supposed to report back anything that we sighted when we were en route to Japan but, of course, we didn't sight anything. But we were so far ahead of them that there was a huge gap between the task force and us. That allowed some of those Japanese fishing boats to move into that gap and one of those fishing boats did penetrate into that area and was sighted by the task force. Halsey was afraid that the fishing boat had sighted the carriers and had reported it by radio to Japan, so they had to launch the bombers early before they had planned to. They planned to launch them, I think about 300 or 400 miles off of the coast of Japan. And as it turned out, they had to launch around 600 miles off the coast, farther away and earlier than scheduled.

Steve: Did you know at the time that they had launched early?

Deen: No. On the *Trout* we only knew what the planned launch time was. I had been listening periodically to the broadcast radio from Tokyo and even though they were broadcasting in Japanese I would listen in. Well on this one particular morning, this radio station went off the air abruptly. I thought, "That's strange, they don't normally do that." Well it wasn't very long after that until we were informed that the bombers had been launched. Then I knew why the radio station went off the air. The bombing had taken place. Those guys, the flyers, they were scheduled to bomb their targets in Tokyo and then fly to China and land there. But since they had to launch early, a few of them didn't make it, they ran out of gas. Some of them were captured, some of them were executed by Japanese, but most of them, actually, with the help of the Chinese, made it back. We were, of course, pleased that we had done all that we could do to help them.

Steve: Did you return to Pearl after that?

Deen: No, after the raid was over, we were released to conduct a normal submarine war patrol against the Japanese shipping. *Thresher* had a rough time. She attacked, I think, three ships near Tokyo Bay, sank one. She took a beating and darn near sank when a wave came over the conning tower and flooded part of the boat

USS *Thresher* (SS 200) c.1940
https://navalunderseamuseum.org/ [accessed 3/7/2024]

shorting out a number of circuits. She recovered but during another attack a Japanese ship tried to catch her with a giant hook.

Steve: A hook?

Deen: Yes, but they got loose and made out okay. *Trout* though, got along very well. We stayed out there off Kobe for a month or so and in that process, we encountered twelve of Japanese ships, attacked eight out of the twelve, and sank five out of the eight.[6]

Steve: Five ships; that's a good patrol! Now, did you know the outcome of the raid at the time it happened?

Deen: Yes, we had a pretty good patrol. In those days communication was rather sparse, sometimes the only information we could get would be from the Radioman, such as myself, copying commercial Morse code press stations. Back then Reuters and AP and all those commercial press stations would send their information by radio all over the world. I could tune in on that, copy it and so, very often, if I had the time, I'd copy some of that stuff and write up a little ship's newspaper, with these news items. That was about the only way we could get news. Sometimes we'd get some good news and sometimes we'd get nothing but propaganda, you know. So, no we didn't know about the success of the raid. We didn't even know how many planes had made it until we got back to Pearl Harbor. And when we got back to Pearl Harbor, we have been at sea for fifty-four days. But then we began to learn that the raid had had a tremendous impact on Japan. It was a tremendous morale booster for the United States.

Steve: I can only imagine the impact it must have had.

Deen: Look at it this way, Steve. Up until that time, every morning in every newspaper, even in Hawaii as well as in the States, the headlines were always something like, Guam has fallen, the Philippines have fallen, Singapore has fallen; bad news every day. Now all of a sudden, there in the headlines was, "Tokyo Bombed!". It was really alarming to them and encouraging to us. But anyway, that was my first war patrol; in support of that Doolittle Raid. I made eight war patrols on the *Trout*. And I made one more onboard the *Gar*.

Steve: What came next for the *Trout* Mr. Brown?

Deen: The next patrol run I made after the Doolittle raid was the Battle of Midway.[7] After we got back from the Doolittle raid, we went into the naval shipyard at Pearl Harbor because when the war started, even though those boats were new boats, they were not really totally ready for war, Steve. They had things that needed to be done. For instance, you being a Machinist's Mate can appreciate the fact that we had dry mufflers on those diesel engines; four of those diesel engines, 1600 horsepower each with dry mufflers, and on a dark night you could see the, you know, the incandescent hunks of carbon sparks, so to speak, coming out of those engines, you could see that for a mile or more. Big chunks of sparks like that. Couldn't have that during the war, you know? So all of those boats were scheduled to get wet mufflers. Wet mufflers, of course, the sparks were quenched with seawater.

Steve: No, if you are on a stealth mission you would not want to be sending up sparks at night.

Deen: Exactly. Also, radar had just come out and the *Trout* was to get a radar. In order to get a radar, they had to cut another hole in the hull and install the mast. In addition, the engineers had torn down two or three of the diesel engines because they had cracked piston liners and they had to replace those. So here we were all torn up in the shipyard, hole in the hull and everything, the captain was summoned over to headquarters, he came back and said, "We're getting underway in twenty-four hours." I couldn't believe it! How could they button that ship up, torn up as it was in the shipyard, and get out of there in **twenty-four hours**? [emphasis his]. I'll tell you, there must have been a hundred and fifty shipyard workers on that damn ship! They welded that hole up for the radar mast, loaded us with torpedoes and stores, and in twenty-four hours, guess what? We got underway on one engine: one main engine! And all hands turned-to and helped the enginemen and we actually finished assembling those engines underway; that was really risky business. You've probably seen these pistons on a Fairbanks Morse diesel engine? This big around. One of those pistons with the connecting rod must have weighed over a hundred pounds. And to have those things rolling around, swinging around, you know, with the boat underway, really you wouldn't want to get in the way of one of them; they'd kill you. So anyway, by the time we got to our assigned patrol station off of Midway, we had all four engines running and on the line.

Steve: That is an amazing feat!

Deen: We did it, but we worked day and night, all hands, to do it. So, we were out in the Battle of Midway for twenty-one days as one of a group of twelve boats. The boats were positioned right around the perimeter of Midway to stop any Japanese invasion force. The boats were stationed this semi-circle of submarines all around the west and southwestern part of Midway. And the idea was if the troopships got in close enough to Midway to where they could land troops, the submarines would sink them. So we were held in that position really as a backup.

Steve: Twelve boats waiting to stop the Japanese invasion fleet.

Deen: That was the plan, which at the time I wasn't too happy about because I wanted to go get 'em but here we were sitting and waiting for them to come to us; but the invasion never materialized. Anyway, the only thing we did there was we picked up a couple of Japanese prisoners, Japanese sailors of course; they were prisoners of war, and we brought them back to Pearl Harbor. But we did not fire a torpedo out there. We spent most of our time diving and dodging our own airplanes because they'd bomb us. They almost sank one of our ships, the *Grayling*.

Steve: That doesn't sound like good planning.

Deen: It wasn't really very well organized because, for one reason, the Army was participating in that whole affair and, well the Army and Navy had never worked together; we couldn't even communicate with each other. They were on different radio frequencies than we were, they had different codes than we had, the whole thing was just very disorganized in that regard. And it was an Army bomber that almost sank the *Grayling*. They saw this submarine and, well, a submarine was a submarine. Bomb that rascal!

Steve: Just too eager! I guess in the situation it's understandable. Mr. Brown, your first two war patrols were two very historically important experiences. What was your next war patrol like?

Deen: My next war patrol, the *Trout's* 5th, we headed for the Solomon Islands and participated in the battle for the Solomon Islands, made a war patrol off of the south of Truk where we were almost sunk. We had to go into Brisbane, Australia which was our closest port for emergency repairs. In fact, we had no gyros. Back then, Steve, the submarines, most of the older submarines including the *Trout* and that class only had one gyrocompass. That was our main navigation device. And our gyro was shattered so we were left without a navigation means. It was bombing from an airplane that caused that damage.[8]

Steve: That sounds awful.

Deen: Well, that was an awful, awful trying, rough period down there. Finally, like I said, they did almost get us and then we had some quite severe damage. Of course, one of the bad things was we really didn't have an accurate way of navigating and when we radioed our situation to COMSUBPAC the *Sailfish*, submarine *Sailfish*, was also there off of Truk, not too far from us. Maybe fifty miles or so away. So they ordered *Sailfish* to break off and escort us into Brisbane. So that's how we got to Brisbane. *Sailfish* was actually the old *Squalus* as you probably know.

Steve: Yes. I do know that. Mr. Brown, I cannot imagine what the experience of being depth charged or having aerial bombs explode near you was like!

Deen: Well, by the time this happened I had had quite a lot of experience from depth charges. Initially, of course, I was scared like everybody else. But then I guess you get sort of battle-hardened; we begin to learn how to gauge how close or how far from us they were. And after a while you sort of just learn to accept it. I didn't really have great fear of them anymore. But when they got real close and they started breaking light bulbs, and glass on gages and things like that, then that was a little worrisome. But then I woke up one morning and I thought, I'm merely being foolish. If I'm standing here and I heard that blasted thing go off, I'm okay; it didn't kill me. I don't have to worry about it 'cause it's spent and it's gone. The one I have to worry about is the one I haven't even heard. That's the next one. So, I got along pretty good that way, you know.

Steve: Very rational response to a terrifying situation.

Deen: Well, when we were bombed it was by that plane off of Truk, it was unanticipated and instantaneous and so close that it just knocked the hell out of us and then it was over with.

Steve: Were you on the surface?

Deen: No, we were submerged at periscope depth. The water there in that area, Steve, is so clear that those Japanese pilots, the fliers, could see us, say at down at one hundred feet depth. The water would be absolutely beautiful it was so clear but that didn't help us. Every day they were dropping bombs on us if we would come up even close to periscope depth. Almost every time we could expect to be bombed. We had a rough time down there. They bombed us in the daytime and at nighttime, the surface craft would trail us, you know, looking for us and we'd have to dive. We'd have trouble staying up long enough to get a full battery charge. But finally we got smart. For some reason or other those Japanese, especially those patrol boats which were something like one of our PC's you know?[9] They never looked aft in their wake. And so, when we discovered that, we would fall in a mile behind them or so in their wake and just follow them around! That way we could get in a battery charge.

Steve: That's ingenious! Still terrifying, but ingenious.

Deen: So, that was my fourth war patrol. After that we made several more war patrols. We finally made it around from Brisbane around to the west coast of Australia into Freemantle and Perth, and we operated out of there. And we'd go into the Philippines, go through the Balabac Strait and also the Sulu Sea and into the Philippines. That was a dangerous run controlled all the way by Japanese, you know, controlled by Japanese airplanes, and so forth. And on occasion we'd take Army Special Forces, which were really guerrilla fighters, we'd take them into the Philippines, unload them and unload ammunition and then explosives and medicine and things that the Filipino freedom fighters needed. And so we made several runs into the Philippines doing that. When the war was over with Japan, the Philippine government awarded us a Philippine Presidential Unit Citation.

Steve: It sounds like it was well deserved.

Deen: So, on one of those trips we brought out three escaped American prisoners of war.[10] Actually, we were supposed to bring out four, but the fourth one, who was an Army lieutenant elected to stay back, stay behind, stay back with the Filipinos and to help them organize and to fight the Japanese. I don't know what ever happened to him. But we brought out the other three, one of them was an Army Air-Force captain. He had been a squad leader for a squadron of P-38 fighters that were stationed in the Philippines; his name was William Dyess. If you've ever heard of Dyess Air Force Base which is down near Abilene, Texas, it's named after him. We brought out an Army major, infantry guy, and he had a scar across his face. It started here, went right down across his face and ended here. A Japanese soldier tried to behead him with a bolo knife and he ducked and all he did was cut his face open, you know. And then we had a Navy lieutenant commander and he told me at the time that he had been communications officer on a cruiser down there, which I think was the *Marblehead*, and I believed him at the time.

Steve: That almost sounds like a movie script.

Deen: Well, after the war I found out who he really was, this lieutenant commander. See we had this cryptographic unit in the Philippines called Station CAST and they were breaking the Japanese code. He was one of those guys, but he never, ever, told; he didn't let the Japanese know what his expertise really was. [11] They would have tortured and beheaded him. But the real important part of that story is the fact that President Roosevelt wanted some first-hand information about the atrocities that the Japanese military was committing against our P.O.W.'s. There were lots of rumors and second-hand information and so forth. But he had no one that had actually been there or took part in it. Now these three guys could. So, when we finally got them back here, they went to Washington and the lid blew off of everything, all over the world. The Japanese were accused of murdering our P.O.W.'s, mistreating them, starving them, you know, the whole nine yards. I was told by some of our P.O.W.s that I served with after the war, that their treatment improved considerably after that.

Steve: Your mission had a great impact.

Deen: That one sure did but again, we didn't quite know it at the time. Then our other war patrols were, most of them were routine except one. On one occasion, in the Makassar Strait, we torpedoed a Japanese tanker, and we blew it in two; it was split in the middle and separated.[12] Oh, you know, that early in the war, Steve, torpedoes were scarce. There was a shortage of them, and, also, you probably know that, on top of that, a lot of them were defective. We were plagued with that for over two years.

Steve: I had heard that. That effected the *Trout* as well?

Deen: Oh yes. It was awful. You know, the principle advantage of a submarine is their stealth. The instant we fired one of those dud torpedoes we gave ourselves away, and we did no damage to the enemy, and then they were free to pounce on us, and beat us up good, and they did, every time. You know?

Steve: Right.

Deen: So, anyway, we blew this tanker's bow off and my captain at that time was Lawson P. Ramage, "Red Ramage". He was one of the seven submariner Medal of Honor recipients. He decided, well, we'll just finish that tanker off with the deck gun and save a torpedo. Well we got in too close and they had machine guns on board and they turned those machine guns on, on the gun crew and raked the deck with machine gun fire. They shot seven of our men, but luckily none of them lost their life. We were almost out of range of the machine guns so the bullets were hitting them low. But one guy lost his leg. The bullet shattered his knee and so his leg had to be amputated.[13]

Steve: Did they do that operation on the boat?

Deen: No, no, the doc patched him up and, along with the other guys that were shot. And, of course, the challenge for the doc then was to avoid infection. The sanitation, you know, on those little submarines was not good. So, and we didn't have penicillin then; in fact we hadn't even heard of it. But anyway, the doc did his job real good. By the time we got into Brisbane, which was several weeks later, the guys that just had flesh wounds, they'd healed up and they were fine. But this fellow who had his knee shattered we had to transfer him to the hospital and they amputated his leg. Then we had another fellow that got a bullet in his heel, and shattered his heel. They couldn't rebuild his heel so he was surveyed, he was given a medical survey from the Navy.

Steve: A medical survey? What is that?

Deen: That is an evaluation by the medical corps to determine if a man is medically fit to remain in the Navy. So if not, as in this case, they would be surveyed out and would receive a disability pension.

Steve: Okay. I understand.

Deen: Well in nineteen and forty-three, after the *Trout's* tenth war patrol, I believe it was, we were ordered from Australia to return to the States because we had worn out a lot of the machinery on the boat. Some of the machinery was very badly worn. See, the *Trout* was commissioned in nineteen and forty, and we'd steamed all over the world for four years, you know? So, it was badly in need of an overhaul. Well, we were ordered back to San Francisco, to Mare Island, for an overhaul. We went back to Mare Island, were overhauled there at the Hunter's Point facility. We were there for about three months or so and then we left there and headed back for Pearl Harbor and the war zone. At that time I was a second class Radioman. The chief Radioman had been in the hospital at Oakland Naval Hospital, and he was still there so we headed for Pearl Harbor without him. We got to Pearl Harbor, we took a reserve Radioman aboard to fill out our complement and we were getting ready, we were all loaded, ready to go on war patrol, the *Trout's* eleventh war patrol.

RM2 (SS) Brown with patrol beard
Author's Collection

Steve: So that was your ninth war patrol on the *Trout*?

Deen: If I had gone. One evening, just before we were to get under-way the next morning, here comes the Chief Radioman to report aboard. They flew him out of San Francisco and over to Pearl; that left us with one Radioman more than we needed. Well, we were scheduled to get a new radar. You know, Steve, technology back then was moving ahead very rapidly. New equipment was coming along all the time; IFF and sophisticated radars, and so forth. So, also back then, I might have mentioned that, there were no such things as ET's [electronics technicians], no ET rating so Radioman was the only electronic rate that there was.[14]

Steve: Okay. I didn't realize that.

Deen: We had picked up a third-class reserve Radio Technician, RT; this was the first of the new electronics ratings and eventually turned into the ET rating. Well this fellow was just a youngster and really was learning. So, I was still, me and the other Radioman on the *Trout*, were still responsible, you know, for all the electronic stuff. So, since we were getting this new and sophisticated radar they decided to leave me in port to go to school, to study that thing so we could keep it going, and so forth. So they left me in to go to radar school, and they went on out on their eleventh war patrol.

I was supposed to return to the ship when they came back, but they didn't come back; they never came back. So that's how I missed going on eternal patrol with my shipmates on the *Trout*. I missed going down with the *Nevada* because they sent me to radio school when it was bombed, and I missed going down with the *Trout*, again because I was in school.

Steve: You were very fortunate! School was good to you!

Deen: That's right! That's right!

Steve: Well eight war patrols, though, that seems like an awful lot for one person.

Deen: Well, it's quite a bit, but it's by no means a record. The top number of war patrols, as far as I know, one guy made, was sixteen. A lot of guys made twelve. So I have not broken any records by any means, by making nine.

Steve: Okay, but still a remarkable number. Yes, you had one more on the *Gar*. Isn't that's right.

Deen: Right. That *Gar* mission was really one to lifeguard for pilots, for airmen. And we picked up seven of them. That was when we were invading the island of Peleliu.[15] It was a terrible fight. We picked up seven airmen there that had been shot down off of Peleliu. And we were fairly close in to the island; close enough that sometimes we were within range of their shore batteries.

Steve: Mr. Brown, now was that the only surface action that you saw? That one on the *Trout* with the tanker there?

Deen: Oh no, not at all. All submarines in fact were ordered, during the war, to interdict the supply of rubber, oil, tin, other things, that were materials of war that were precious to the Japanese. They used small boats, small boats like we called them junks although junk is a Chinese word for a small boat, but we called them either sampans or junks. Most of them small wooden ships; maybe they might be a hundred ton, seventy-five ton or whatever. But they had thousands of them, and they were using them to transport a lot of their critical materials to Japan from places like Singapore and Borneo and

Sarawak and so forth. So we were ordered to sink them. Which we did. We sank a lot of them. Let's see, I expect, see when I left the *Trout*, we had sunk a total of twenty six vessels, eleven of which were big ships, and all the rests were those sampans. So there was lots of gun action.

Steve: Was that because those smaller ships weren't really worth a torpedo?

Deen: Yes, just right. You'd sink them with a gun. They often sailed close to shore in shallow water to seek safety. This shallow water was not optimal for a torpedo attack but ideal for surface action with the deck guns. And sometimes, you know, on some of them, we'd sink them, and these bales of rubber, raw rubber would float; you'd see plainly what they were carrying.

Steve: That's curious. Especially considering that more modern submarines abandoned the deck guns in favor of pure stealth and surprise.

Deen: You are right.

Steve: Now how about your activities just when you were onboard, off-duty; I guess you might say your free time? What types of things you might have done for entertainment or fun? I've heard about crews having marathon cribbage games or chess matches or...

Deen: For entertainment we used to play cribbage a lot. Cribbage is a very distinctive submarine game. As you might know, Captain Dick O'Kane's cribbage board is still passed and kept by the oldest boat in the fleet.[16] A lot of boards were made on the boat, you might call it trench art, I think. We'd also play cards, sometimes poker, you know. Especially when we were operating out of Australia; sometimes they'd be a lot of money in a poker game. The reason for that is because a pound note, Australia had the English money system, and a one-pound note was worth three dollars and twenty-five cents. But you get these guys in a poker game and they start playing these one-pound notes like they were one-dollar bills. So, I've seen lots of poker games in the mess hall that probably had way more than a thousand dollars in the pot.

Steve: Wow! That's high stakes!

Deen: Yes, but that really wasn't for me. I kept my money and I still have some! This is a souvenir I had made in Australia. I had this made on the tender; they put my coins and a badge of the Australian military police on the wooden plaque in the shape of Australia.

Wooden Plaque, with Australian Coins and Military Badge
Author's Collection

Steve: That's a great souvenir!

Deen: A reminder of happy times. Anyway, mostly when we played cards, or when we played cribbage, it was generally just for fun, no big money. And along about after six months or a year after the war started we got a movie machine on board. And we'd take a whole stack of movies with us so we could show those movies. Most of the time we'd show them over and over and over, you know, before we got back in.

Steve: Now that would be in crew's mess?

Deen: No, the movies we generally showed in the forward torpedo room. There wasn't enough room to show them in the crew's mess. Too small. So late in the war we had the movies and we always had a radio, a shortwave radio. You could tune that in and listen to whatever news you might be able to hear.

Steve: Would you hear that just in the radio room or throughout the boat?

Deen: No, well, in the beginning it was just in the crew's mess. But then later on, after we got an overhaul, it was throughout the boat. You had speakers throughout the boat and we had a record player; we'd buy a lot of records and we'd trade with different ships.

Steve: How was the mail? Did the mail get through to you?

Deen: It got, generally it got to us pretty good, you know. The only thing is we were not allowed to write anything back, out, that had anything of any significance in it. You know, militarily. Because all of our mail, outgoing mail, was censored. About all you could say is, well, I'm okay, and here I am and…

Steve: Of course. Now you started off in Missouri, but you ended up in Connecticut here. How did that happen?

Deen: Well first I was detached from the *Gar* after that one war patrol. When the *Trout* sunk, I went to the, the squadron office called me and they told me the *Trout* was sunk. The squadron personnel officer told me, "Well, the *Gar* needs a senior Radioman and you're the only one we've got." He said, "If you'll make one patrol run on the *Gar*, when you get back in, I'll send you back to the States to commission a new boat under construction." That sounded like a pretty good deal to me. So I said, "Okay, I'll do that." So that's how I made one run on the *Gar*. And he kept his promise. When we got

back in, sure enough, boom, boy, I was on my way to the States to new construction!

Steve: Was that at Electric Boat here?

Deen: I first reported to Mare Island. Everybody did from the Pacific anyway. I went to Mare Island. They gave me thirty days leave, I think, and then I was to report to Subase New London. I reported in Subase New London and went to the squadron office and the first thing I had to do was to take a physical examination. I

RM-1 (SS) Brown in Pearl Harbor
Author's Collection

went to the hospital and there was a senior medical officer there. He was a captain. There were about fifteen or twenty young recruit sailors, all of them just Sub School students, and I was the only rated guy there and well, I was in my dress uniform. I had all my ribbons and the submarine combat pin on and everything. And he looked at me and the pin and said, "How many war patrols have you made?" I said, "Well captain, I've made nine." He said, "You made nine?" I said, "Yes sir." So he gave me an examination and he said, "You're not making any more." I looked at him, kind of stunned, you know. I said, "Well, does that mean there's something wrong with me?" He said, "You're too nervous." He wouldn't let me go, you know. I think he was saying, "You've done enough." So they put me on a school boat on the river and I was training new students right up until the cease fire in September of '45.

Steve: Do you remember which boat that was?

Deen: Yes. USS *Cachalot*. SS170. We trained student officers as well as enlisted. I did that for about a year onboard the *Cachalot*.

Steve: Now, you were teaching Sub School, but had you ever gone through it yourself?

Deen: No. Remember I was a surface sailor who ended up as a Radioman at the Pearl Harbor Subase because my ship, the *Nevada*, was on the bottom.

Steve: That's right, that's right.

Deen: When I got on the *Trout*, of course they knew that I hadn't been to Sub School, and the Exec told me, he said, "Well, we're going to give you six months. You have to qualify in six months or

USS *Cachalot* (SS 170) c. 1936
Submarine Force Museum & Library Archives

you're gone." I qualified in four months.

Steve: That's quick!

Deen: Well, I couldn't go anywhere, there was no liberty. So all I had to do in my spare time was study the boat, and make diagrams and so forth. All the new guys made up qualification books. I made piping diagrams and wiring diagrams; just about drew out all the boat systems. So, I did all of that and so in four months I was qualified. I liked doing it too. And I had a lot of admiration for those sub men. I guess I wanted to learn myself up to their level.

Steve: Did you keep your qualification books?

Deen: No, they are gone. I was only going to the radar school for a short while; you know, I was only transferred temporarily. So, I left them on the boat; them and some of my other things. All that went down with the boat, down with all my shipmates.

Steve: Do you still think about the *Trout* and your friends onboard?

Deen: Steve, I think about them all the time.

Steve: Of course...of course. Mr. Brown, what made you decide to stay in the Navy?

Deen: By the time the war was over with I was, you know, like, six years in. And so, I decided to finish it up.

Steve: I know in the Army, of course they had way more men than they needed for peacetime, so it was hard to stay in. Was that true in the Navy as well?

Deen: Only for certain rates. They had an excess of Torpedomen, and they had an excess of Enginemen, and Gunner's Mates; they had too many of them. But mostly Torpedomen and Enginemen in submarines. And, uh, you either had to go out of the Navy or change your rate in order to stay in. And, also, there was very little chance that you would be advanced.

Steve: Right.

Deen: But that problem also permeated all the ranks. Like I was hung up as first-class petty officer for several years because they would not allow any more promotions to chief, you know.

Steve: Okay. What made you decide to make Connecticut your home?

Deen: Well, I did some duty here locally on a couple of different submarines on the river, you know, after the war. Like I told you about my duty on the old school boat, the *Cachalot*, and then, when the war ended, we had taken the *Cachalot* down to the Philadelphia Navy Yard because we wore out all the vent valve operating mechanisms and we could hardly dive the boat, you know. We had to repair those. Well, the war ended while we were in Philadelphia and *Cachalot* was an old, old, submarine. It was commissioned in 1933, I believe, and it wasn't really up to date. So as soon as the cease fire took place, we got word, hey, you won't be repaired, you're going to be scrapped; the boat's going to be decommissioned. So everybody was transferred back to New London. That was right after VJ Day [August 15, 1945].

I got to New London, and they put me onboard the submarine *Spikefish*. The hull number was 404. And so I spent three years on it.

And then I was transferred from *Spikefish* to the Admiral's staff. And that was a very good job I thoroughly enjoyed. That's one of the reasons why I elected to stay. I spent a tour of duty on the Admiral's staff and in 1952 or so

USS *Spikefish* (SS 404) c.1944
*Submarine Force Museum
& Library Archives*

the Navy begin to build up again because of the Korean War. And Submarine Squadron Ten was re-commissioned and the submarine tender Fulton was re-commissioned to take care of Squadron Ten. I was offered the job as squadron Chief Radioman to re-commission Submarine Squadron Ten and that was a good job, so I took that. So, I had some real good assignments there late in my career.

Steve: Sounds like it. Now can I ask you, did you, during wartime, did you know, did you know your wife, had you met her yet?

Deen: No. I was not married and had not met her yet. We did not get married until 1947. But I wouldn't get married during the war. There were a lot of guys that would not. It was very plain that submarine business was a very risky business. One of the riskiest businesses in the military.

Steve: Right.

Deen: Our losses, you know, were the highest of any military unit. I had no inclination, whatsoever, to leave a widow. I wouldn't get married.

Steve: I'd have to agree. Not the same situation as yours but I felt the same way. I also didn't get married until I got out of the Navy. It was actually two weeks after!

Deen: Isn't that something!

Steve: Back to the boats, old and new, the crews seemed to weld themselves into a single unit. Would you agree with that?

Deen: Well, that's very true especially in the older boats. We were not so compartmented as they are today. And we had requirements back then that are entirely different from what they are today. For instance, when we qualified submarines, back in the old days, you had to know how to operate every major system on the boat, it didn't matter what it was. Whether it was torpedoes, the engines, the propulsion plant, you had to do it all. Well, they don't do that anymore. You qualify in the area where you work, and where it entails your job.

Steve: When I qualified in '79 you had to understand, at least, the concept, like with the sonar and whatnot, and radio. There's no way you could know how to operate it but you had to know what was in there, what it did, what the power supply was, and what to do with it in an emergency.

Deen: Well, there were certain things that we did not have to know how to operate like I did not operate the Torpedo Data Computer [TDC]. That's quite complicated. But the major systems on the boat, yes, I had to operate those. Not only know what they did but know how to operate them. I could go back and start a diesel engine or start all the diesel engines. I could run the propulsion plant if I had to. I could even fire a torpedo if I had to fire a torpedo. But they don't do that anymore. Now they may identify, have a sailor identify what they are but we had to operate them. But the ship was much smaller and wasn't so complex as they are today. Today they're much too complex for one man to know everything on the ship. You couldn't do that. So they don't do that.

Steve: It seems like if you're in a situation like that and you know that you can depend on every man on board...

Deen: That's right. We could almost replace every man onboard, you know, if something happened to him. I could not replace the fire control man because I wouldn't know how to operate the TDC, Torpedo Data Computer. But as far as a throttle man on the, in the engine room, or engineer, yeah, I could step right in there and do that. They couldn't come to the radio room and operate the radio (laughter). That was not essential to the safety of the ship anyway.

Steve: Now what, what was your battle station?

Deen: Well, very often I'd be on the sonar during battle stations if we were submerged. Now if we went to battle stations on the surface I'd probably be on the radar.

Steve: Okay. Would that be up on the ...

Deen: In the Conning Tower.

Steve: Was there sonar maybe, or radar equipment that was forward on the torpedo room?

Deen: Well, there was quite a bit of sonar equipment on, say, the old fleet boats that was in the forward torpedo room. And one of the sonars, in particular, was manually trained. You've probably seen a lot of pictures of a thing up on deck, forward, that looked like the letter "T". Well, that whole thing rotated, that was the sonar. It was one of the early, early, sonar arrays as you might say. And yeah, so you had a wheel down there so you could rotate that thing. And then there were two sound heads that were mounted on masts, shafts, if you will, they penetrated the bottom of the submarine. You raised and lowered them hydraulically. You could, in an emergency, train them. And they were very, very hard to manually train if you had to. Normally they were trained electrically.

Steve: Okay.

Deen: Yeah, but in fleet boats that's all that I can actually remember that was in the forward torpedo room. Now our first radar was in the, the antennae and the whole radar thing was installed in the Conning Tower. But the antennae was also manually trained. You had a gear, a gear mechanism, you had a crank, a wheel with a crank on it. You stood there looking at the radar and you were cranking all the time. You know, watching the radar screen.

Steve: That sounds difficult.

Deen: Yes, but eventually it was motorized, and became very much different. The first radar we had, you know, did not give you direction; it gave you range only. You didn't know where the guy was but you knew how far he was so it was a help! And it was designed for detecting aircraft. It was not a surface-search radar. So it was a help. And we didn't care where the airplane was just wanted to know if he was there. (laughter)

Steve: And get down.

Deen: Right! But that didn't last very long because it was primitive by today's standards. And it didn't take the Japanese very long to build countermeasures for it. And as soon as we turned that thing on it was just like a beacon to them. They knew right exactly where we were (laughs). And pretty soon here come the planes, right after us. We soon learned we couldn't run that thing very long or they'd be on us, yeah.

Steve: I read this book titled *Iron Coffins*.

Deen: Yeah. Great book.

Steve: Oh, it is. Very readable. Werner.

Deen: Herbert Werner.

Steve: Yes, and he's talking about I think the same thing. The German radar which was like a beacon. And really helped out the Allied anti-submarine efforts.

Deen: Absolutely. That's right. I met him...

Steve: Oh, no kidding!

Deen: ...and had quite a long chat with him. He became a citizen, you know, of this country.

Steve: I didn't know that. What an opportunity to speak with him.

Deen: Yes. And he lived down in New Jersey. Well, after I retired from the Navy, I spent twenty-four years at Electric Boat. I was in engineering there, electronic engineering. We had, what you'd call, a management club dinner. And Werner was the principal speaker. So, I was lucky enough to spend some time with him and talk with him, you know, about his operations and mine, the similarities, and dis-similarities.

Steve: Right. Oh, that's fabulous.

Deen: He wrote a fantastic book. Very, very well written, simply written, and understandable, and he told it like it was.

Steve: I agree. Right. Even though he was a German submarine captain I found his experiences and insights very relevant to my experiences.

Deen: Exactly right. Oh, one thing I want to show you.

Steve: What's that?

Deen: Well, the Doolittle Raiders would have reunions, I guess you'd say, and sometimes they would meet in our area. So towards the end of that organization, I was honored to receive this award from Lt. Col. Richard E. Cole; he was Doolittle's co-pilot. It seems, at the time I got this, he was the last flyer alive that participated and I was the last submariner.

B-25B award plane model
Author's Collection

Deen Brown receiving award plane from Lt. Col. Richard Cole
Author's Collection

Steve: Wow! Right from Doolittle's co-pilot! That's something!

Deen: I was quite pleased to receive it.

Steve: As you should have been. Mr. Brown, let me ask you, do you ever regret finding your way into the submarine service?

Deen: Not for a second. I miss the men I'll never see again and the ones that are leaving us every day now, but I loved every minute of the experience. No, it was very plain that submarine business was a very risky business. One of the most risky businesses in the military. During the war our losses were close to 25%, boats and men. But we never had any trouble manning the boats; volunteers would do anything to get onboard a boat headed for the war zone. Some even stowed away!

Steve: It's amazing to me that such a dangerous, difficult, and demanding assignment had men do almost anything to get a billet on a wartime submarine. Can you explain that kind of fierce motivation?

Deen: Well, Steve, you were on the boats, though much after me, but I think you experienced a lot of what drew men to the submarine life. It was demanding for certain, but one thing I liked about the submarine Navy was, number one, it was not "Spit and Polish" regulation. Like in the battleship Navy, sailors will spend half the day shining brightwork so the captain's railings on his ladders would look good or something like that. That, to me, that was an awful waste of manpower. Submarine guys had something real to do. Meaningful. And that's what meant a lot to me; I wanted to do something meaningful and real; never mind the spit and polish. So that was one of the things about the submarine duty that I liked. And it was a challenge. I say, you know, submarining is a dangerous business; it's dangerous today. The sea is an unforgiving place to be. So, you know, you put it all together, and you sort of get the idea, I think, after a while, that you're accomplishing something worthwhile, you know. And in the war we were always on the front line; you didn't have to wonder if you were making a difference; the sound of an enemy freighter, filled with the materials of war, breaking up and heading for the bottom let you know instantly that you were making a difference.

Steve: That's very well said Mr. Brown.

We continued the interview shifting our conversation around between the new and old Navy, different experiences, and books we had both read on the submarine warfare. After I had concluded the interview and the recorder was off, I was heading out the door when Mr. Brown stopped me and said one final thing. It was so unexpected, and it touched me so profoundly, that I wrote it down as soon as I got to my car. Mr. Brown said,

"Steve, I fought the war for years after the war was over."

Deen Brown saluting the Lost Boat flags at the National Submarine Memorial – East, Memorial Day observance, 2015.
Editor's Photo

CHAPTER 2

THE TIP OF THE SPEAR

USS *Trout* (SS-202) in the South Pacific in 1942
by J. "Deen" Brown, RMCM(SS), USN(Ret.)

USS *Trout* (SS 202), 11 December 1943
Submarine Force Museum & Library Archives

SETTING THE SCENE

THE *TREATY OF Versailles* that ended the war between Germany and the Allied Powers was signed on June 28, 1919. The treaty assigned to the Empire of Japan a number of island groups in the South Pacific formerly held by Imperial Germany. Among these were the Marshalls, the Marianas (less Guam), and the Caroline Territories. "The Mandates" was a common way of referring to this collection of islands. Instead of aiding the indigenous people of these islands to improve their living conditions, as was mandated, the Japanese wasted no time moving in and aggressively fortifying these lands. This military build-up fit in perfectly with the Japanese imperialist concept known as *The Greater East Asia Co-Prosperity Sphere*. This concept purported to extend the Japanese area of influence beyond East Asia and promote the cultural and economic unity of Northeast Asians, Southeast Asians, and Oceanians. In reality it was a plan to create a self-sufficient "bloc of Asian nations led by the Japanese and free of Western powers."[17] Though not overtly stated in this concept, the conquest of Australia and New Zealand, with their rich and plentiful land masses, was clearly the intent of Japanese strategists. Absorbing those countries into the growing Japanese hegemony would deny the United States important allies and crucial advance bases in any future conflict. This strategic defensive weakening of the U. S. and its allies would be an important prerequisite to their ultimate plan: destroy the United States' naval forces based in the Hawaiian Islands, acquire that island group, and remove the Americans as contenders in the dominance of the Pacific.

The Caroline Islands consisted of a widely scattered group of about five hundred islands; one of the largest of these was the Truk Atoll. In the case of Truk, the land mass did not provide the principal Japanese interest in this real estate, the real value lay in the atoll's lagoon. Truk Lagoon was of significant size, had deep water, and water protected from the natural destructive forces of the Pacific by a reef and higher surrounding lands. Two passages allowed large, deep draft vessels to negotiate the reef from both the north and south end of the lagoon. During the years before World War II, Japan poured vast levels of military equipment into a well-planned base at Truk that could support their fleets and smaller bases on any of the neighboring island possessions. Truk would also become the Japanese headquarters for the Southern Pacific, in some way their own "Pearl Harbor." During this buildup, U. S. and Allied military analysts viewed the Japanese treaty violations with growing concern. Based on their aggressive actions, the Japanese intentions were clear.

Once the war in the Pacific began, the strategic importance of the Japanese base at Truk could not be denied. In 1942 leading Navy officials including Admirals Earnest King, Chief of Naval Operations, Chester Nimitz, Commander of the Pacific Fleet, and Robert English, Commander Submarine Forces – Pacific, planned a military attack against this heavily defended base. If successful, the attack would at least diminish the base's effectiveness and ultimately destroy it completely. At the time this was in planning, the strength of the Japanese Navy in the Pacific was measurably greater than the Allied navies. To undertake such a major campaign against a superior foe would require a large collection of aircraft, submarines, and many supporting surface ships all of which would take time to acquire, equip, train, and assemble. If the campaign were compared to a spear, the tip of the spear would be the submarines. These stealthy warships could enter enemy territory where a conspicuous surface naval force could not. Until the massing and building of invasion fleet could be accomplished, the subs had to take the lead. The subs would perform two functions; they would report on the actual presence of enemy warships and then attack and sink the same.

USS *Trout* (SS-202) in the South Pacific

In June of 1942 the USS *Trout* (SS-202), on which I was a crewmember, entered the Pearl Harbor Navy Shipyard to undergo needed repairs and alterations and, most importantly, to get our first new surface search radar. That new electronic system was exciting to us because it would allow us to "see targets in the dark!" In late August, 1942, *Trout* was repaired and altered and fully loaded with food, fuel, and torpedoes; she was ready for her fifth war patrol which was to be an extended one. She also had a new Commanding Officer, one LCDR L. P. "Red" Ramage. After the patrol, instead of heading back to Pearl, *Trout* would go to her new squadron headquarters now based onboard the USS *Pelias* (AS-14) at Fremantle, Perth, Western Australia.

After topping off fuel tanks at Midway Island we headed south. The long cruise to the Carolines was uneventful except for a welcome visit by a lone albatross. That bird landed onboard, rode us for a day, and at least left us a seaman's good omen. In early September, as we approached the equator, the crew began to notice the sea had become crystal clear with a beautiful blue hue. It looked so inviting more than one of us expressed the urge to take a dip! Little did we know then what stress and peril that clear water would cause us to endure. Captain Ramage informed us that he had been warned about intense antisubmarine activity in the area around Truk. As we approached the vicinity around the islands it was clear that his intel was spot-on. During daylight it was common to see up to three patrol boats (SC's) in the south "Otta" Pass area where we were patrolling; constant alertness was the order of the day.

USS *Pelias* in Fremantle 1944

Drawing, Charcoal on Paper; by LCDR.
Griffith Baily Coale, USNR; 1944, Public Domain image,
http://www.navsource.org/archives/09/36/3614.htm
[accessed 3/6/2024].

The vigilant daylight hours were spent submerged which meant that we ended the day with the propulsion plant batteries near depletion. To keep the ship operating we would surface at dark and begin charging batteries which took four to six hours of continuous charge time. During the charge we were often interrupted by the ever-present patrol boats and forced to dive. This hit-and-miss battery charging was frustrating not to mention it created concern for the boat's safety but we would "low-ball" any talk of that. The captain was also frustrated with this situation and he decided we would not keep playing "tag" with the patrol boats but instead try a "follow the leader" game. During the night he'd take position about three-quarters of a mile behind a patrol boat and follow its course. If the PC changed direction, we would follow, matching his every turn and visually obscured by his wake, and we continued this until our batteries were fully charged. The captain's sensible but outlandish idea worked quite well. Apparently, our presence was partly hidden by the disturbed sea of the PC, the noise of his own engines. The Japanese sailors seemed to exclusively focus their search attentions directly ahead, paying little attention to the area of their wake.

Our confidence was buoyed by knowing that we could have a "full" battery; that buoy would soon sink a little as a more severely threatening situation occurred and the crystal clear water was the troublemaker. We were submerged in bright daylight at periscope depth: about fifty-eight feet and the sea state was quite calm. *Trout* was suddenly jolted by two nearby explosions a few seconds apart. The periscopes were not up and showing above the surface which added to the mystery of our apparent discovery as it was clear those bombs came from an aircraft. What wasn't apparent at the time was that in that clear water a plane flying overhead could see our submarine silhouette when we were at periscope depth. The danger of detection by these aerial bombers impaired our advantage of stealth. Since we clearly could not remain at periscope depth for very long, our periscope scans of the surface were quick and dangerous, and followed by our prompt return to the safety of deep water.

We remained in an area fifty to seventy miles southwest of the Otta Lagoon pass. On September 28th a periscope scan detected a distant ship. Soon after another ship appeared nearby and a few minutes later, two more; the first ships were destroyers and the second pair were cruisers. Patience was in order! Naval reasoning indicated they were escorting a large warship, a battleship or aircraft carrier, so these escort ships were allowed to pass unmolested. A large ship finally appeared; it was an aircraft carrier and that would be our target. The carrier was in a reasonable attack position and the *Trout* was ready and waiting. At 1405 we fired five torpedoes. A large explosion occurred, followed by a second. All eyes went to the Firecontrolman with his stopwatch; the run time was correct: the target was struck! The remaining three mysteriously gave no sign of abnormal behavior or of a mishap; they simply disappeared. The captain on the periscope said the carrier was on fire; smoke and flames were rolling over the flight deck. One of the cruisers was making much black smoke indicating it had put on flank speed to clear out without concern for tell-tale smoke. The captain ordered "take her down!" as a destroyer was headed straight for *Trout* "with a bone in its mouth." As we descended depth charges were exploding but, since none of them were close, our descent continued unabated. At three-hundred feet we leveled off; effects and sounds of depth charges were felt and heard for about an hour before they abruptly stopped. An inspection of the *Trout* revealed no damage. After evening darkness we surfaced and determined the area was "all-clear" so we headed to a new patrol area.

Trout returned to her regular routine of keeping clear of patrol boats and sighting an occasional aircraft. While making a morning navigational fix in preparation for a close reconnoiter of Otta Pass the boat lurched and rolled to starboard from a tremendous explosion. Aerial bombs had scored! A man in the Chief's Room was thrown from his bunk and another knocked to the deck in the Torpedo Room. We were all stunned by the violence and suddenness of the attack. The Control Room Chief instinctively flooded tanks sending the boat downward. As the boat passed eighty feet another bomb went off but it had little effect. When the boat leveled off a thorough inspection was made for leaks and damage. The periscope hull seals were both leaking into the Conning Tower rendering their use in question. Also, the full-size hatch located at the rear end of the Conning Tower was leaking and spraying sea water onto people and equipment. The water was draining down to the Pump Room bilge where the pump was able to send it overboard. Other more minor leaks were quickly stopped and broken light bulbs replaced; the hull was deemed seaworthy.

After dark we surfaced to perform a topside inspection. Both periscopes were clearly out of commission and part of the radar antennae was blown away. Below decks, our technicians continued to work on the gyrocompass, which had been running poorly, but this attack finished it off. The gyro was our principal instrument for navigation. The gyro and the periscopes worked together to provide data to the Torpedo Data Computer (TDC); without these important sensors our ability to perform a torpedo attack was unlikely. The captain sent a radio message to our sub force commander informing him of our plight. In a few hours he received orders; discontinue patrol and proceed to Brisbane, East Australia, for repairs.

Navigating using a simple magnetic compass on a steel ship is fraught with bearing error. En route, frequent celestial fixes were taken to verify our assumed geographic position. Writing this more than seventy-four years later I admit that my memory of our navigation challenges during this period has become blurred. However, in my mind I still believe that the USS *Sailfish* (SS-192), formerly the *Squalus*, was ordered to rendezvous with *Trout* and escort us to Brisbane. The war patrol reports from neither submarine mention that this occurred nor is there any other substantiating documentation currently available but I remember that *Trout* and *Sailfish* were together in Brisbane.[18]

USS *Sailfish* (SS-192), off the Mare Island Navy Yard, Vallejo, California,
13 April 1943
Submarine Force Museum & Library Archives

AT HOME IN BRISBANE

Cruising up the Brisbane River to the dock area was a pleasant
experience. Spring-like weather had arrived and the land was an
inviting, lush green. Crowds of people on the river bank were yelling,
waving, and cheering us on. These greetings were our first introduction to Australian hospitality that remained with us throughout our
brief stay there. In the early evening I joined two shipmates heading
to the uptown to see a little of Brisbane City. As we passed through
a sentry gate guarding New Farm Wharf we encountered a crowd of
local people standing nearby. They variously invited us to come to
dinner in their home, or to join them at a party or accompany them
to some sporting event; a very hospitable greeting.

We had to decline since we had promised some of our own shipmates that we would join them at the Lennon Hotel for a beer and to talk over our latest experiences. Much of our discussion that evening revolved around our suspicion that our torpedoes were not fully reliable. We had raised this same subject on the boat at times but the officers would not discuss the matter, believing it was bad for morale, so it was low-balled. In the mind of some, their silence tended to exacerbate the matter.

The next afternoon I went to the city again to shop for some personal items and souvenirs. Since I was in uniform I was easily identifiable as an American. A similar crowd again invited me to all sorts of events but I wanted to do my shopping so I politely declined. When we left Pearl I knew we were changing homeport to our new forward base in Fremantle, Australia and that we would be there for an extended time, perhaps one or two years. Even with that forewarning, I neglected to familiarize myself with the British currency system and understand the exchange rates. When shopping, I was embarrassed that I didn't know what anything cost since the prices were in British Pounds. So I would choose an item, hold out my hand with money, and ask the clerk to take what it cost. That worked out fine and, in addition, often resulted in a cheerful conversation. Also, girls who worked in the shop would gather around me and teach me to count their money. I was a slow learner.....

Our delightful visit to Brisbane eventually came to an end. The submarine tender USS *Griffin* had finished the major repairs of all our bomb damage. *Trout* was now whole again with new periscopes, gyro compass and radar antennae. That sprung leaky rear Conning Tower hatch had been fully welded shut [newer subs being built would not have this hatch there so no great hardship.] We departed on October 17th for Fremantle, Perth, our assigned base in Western Australia. Three days out we received a radio message to return immediately to Brisbane, which we did, and arrived there on October 23rd. In wartime plans change frequently and, back in Brisbane, they had prepared for our arrival. All remaining repairs were completed, mostly by us but with assistance from the tender, as materials for a war patrol came pouring aboard; torpedoes, fuel, oil, and food in all the quantities we could carry. Much of the food was simply stacked topside where it was when we cast off on the afternoon of October 26th. Men were passing stores below as the boat navigated out of Brisbane harbor. All finally shipshape, we went below and were back to war.[19]

Once underway our captain explained our orders. We were going to the Solomon Islands. A battle for Guadalcanal was in process and ongoing and we were to join that battle. Our trip to station was uneventful but after about a week there things became very active and at times perplexing.

On November 13th, shortly after arriving at our patrol station, *Trout* was patrolling on line with *Flying Fish* and *Grampus* about eighty miles north of Indispensible Straits. We had received a message reporting the position of an enemy battleship headed towards us so we were on the lookout. About 0700 escorting destroyers were sighted and passed and about half an hour later a battleship came into view. We closed to about 6000 yards when the BB turned away. The rest of the morning and most of the afternoon was spent avoiding destroyers (DDs) and aircraft while we searched for the battleship. We sighted her again around 1500 emerging from a rain squall and closed to 1,800 yards. *Trout* launched five torpedoes at the battleship which we identified as *Kirishima*, one of Japan's older battleships. Waiting to hear an explosive hit seemed like minutes even though it was less than sixty seconds. Though the hoped for sound of our own torpedoes was not heard we got our explosions soon enough. A pattern of depth charges was rained down on us by an angry destroyer. The destroyer's attack was intense, but brief, and when all seemed clear we surfaced and transmitted a position report on the enemy force's position.[20]

The captain received a radio response about Guadalcanal being shelled by naval gunfire. His feeling of guilt about the unsuccessful attack was evident when he wrote that our soldiers had been shelled "all because we failed."[21] She escaped us but the *Kirishima* would not survive this battle. After inflicting damage on the American battleship USS *South Dakota* the *Kirishima* was attacked by another of our new battleships, the USS *Washington*, which had evaded the Japanese fleet to get into point-blank position. The *Washington's* sixteen-inch guns blasted *Kirishima* into a mangled pile of steel. The Japanese cruiser *Nagara* initially tried to tow *Kirishima* out of Ironbottom Sound but, after realizing the extent of the damage, *Kirishima* was left to sink. When we heard about this later we were glad that a major enemy ship had been destroyed but our morale took a blow when we realized that we had a shot at sinking the same ship but blew it perhaps because of faulty dud torpedoes! How long would we have to fight with ineffective weapons!?

Many ship contacts were made but the situation was often mixed-up and confusing. This early in the war our subs lack an electronic identification system (IFF: Identification Friend or Foe) to help with target identity, i.e. who was friend and who was foe.[22] Thus identity determination was strictly visual and often imperfect. When Japanese and United States ships mixed, friendly targets were sometimes attacked and valid attacks on targets withheld. During the dark early morning hours of November 15th we were on the surface charging batteries when a large searchlight suddenly illuminated us. Seconds later two salvos whizzed a few feet over our deck and landed twenty yards past us. The captain secured all engines and went to ahead-emergency and dived to two hundred feet but that destroyer (DD) was right on us. The captain remarked that it might be one of our own DD "considering the speed and precision with which they handled the situation."[23] As the depth charges came down he was proved right. The nature of the exploding sound told us that they were definitely American; they exploded with a single "Boom." One could hear the Japanese depth charges arm ("Click") just before exploding ("Boom"). We had heard plenty of that distinct two-part sound, Click-Boom! But now we were being attacked by a "friendly" ship? In the midst of this the captain ordered a red signal flare released. The depth charge attack stopped and the DD's sonar began tapping out a request for us to surface in Morse code. Once we were on the surface they came close and asked if we were okay and did we need help. Or reply was no, only our feelings were hurt and ruffled. We parted and went our own ways.

Trout departed Guadalcanal late on November 18th. Many crewmen thought we were finally destined for Fremantle, Perth where we were supposed to be. Next, however, another wartime plan change. We were headed back to Brisbane for a brief stop for supplies and repairs. The depth charges, both enemy and friendly, had left one periscope again useless. We ended our sixth war patrol on November 23rd as we arrived at the New Farm Wharf Base in Brisbane. The scene at the base had totally changed. The previous sub-tender, Griffin, was gone and two newly built tenders had taken over: the USS *Fulton* (AS-11) and the USS *Sperry* (AS-12). These ships were awe inspiring; their graceful lines and form resembled those of a commercial passenger liner. *Sperry* quickly finished our few needed repairs. On November 28th we were underway again and headed to Fremantle. It seemed we had surely taken a "long-way" around getting to West Australia. We left Pearl Harbor in August of 1942, completed two successful war patrols, damaged a major enemy capital ship, been depth charged by our own destroyer, and fended off the effects of severe damage and major leaks before we could cast our mooring lines at our home base. We arrived at Fremantle harbor on December 8th and moored alongside the USS *Pelias* (AS-14), our tender and Squadron Headquarters.

While we were there it became common knowledge that "Red" Ramage had a "heated" discussion with senior naval officials about suspected torpedo failures, erratic runs, premature detonations, and failure to run. This was some talk that his "discussion" became so "heated" that the Admiral had him removed from the *Pelias*. No harm done. Eventually, enough sub captains had enough heated discussions that the high command finally took the matter seriously and found a way to fix our faulty torpedoes. How many men remain on eternal patrol because of those duds I don't like to think about.

We received some interesting information about the aircraft carrier we attacked south of Truk; she was the *Taiyō*. *Taiyō* was laid down in 1940 as the ocean liner *Kasuga Maru* but before she was completed she was requisition by the Japanese military as a supply and personnel transport. *Kasuga Maru* worked at this until mid-1941 when she was converted into an escort carrier; this Japanese class of escort carriers were larger than American escort carriers. The new warship would have a straight flight deck with elevators but no island or catapults. The *Taiyō* was used as a training ship, aircraft transporter and as convoy escort. The ship survived our torpedo attack, made it back to Truk, and thence to Japan for major damage repair. Our Navy officials informed us that *Trout* was the first U. S. submarine to torpedo and damage an enemy aircraft carrier in the war.

In late November 1943, *Trout* proceeded to the U. S. A. for a much needed major overhaul. Our Speed of Advance (SOA) was impaired due to the infirmities of our machinery. Additionally, most men aboard had been deployed abroad for near three years.

As we approached California, the captain allowed three or four men at a time to the bridge to view the shores of our homeland. I shall always remember the inspiring view. The Golden Gate Bridge loomed majestically across the San Francisco Bay above a fog bank. Thoughts of home, family, and friends were firm in my mind. At last we were home! Home to God and country and, for a while, separated from strife, death, and destruction.

EPILOGUE – *TAIYŌ'S* WHOLE STORY

Imperial Japanese Navy's aircraft carrier, *Taiyō*
in harbor at Yokosuka, Japan, c. September 1943.
Public Domain image

Taiyō was restored and returned to service after her encounter with *Trout*. She seemingly became a favorite target for the American submarines. USS *Tunny* (SS-282) torpedoed her on April 9, 1943 and USS *Cabrilla* (SS-288) had a go at her on September 24, 1943. After each time *Taiyō* was repaired and put back into service. Not until the USS *Rasher's* (SS-269) big night on August 18, 1944 did the *Taiyō* meet her end. Though the Japanese sailors believed their ship was blessed by divine wind spirits or *kamikaze*, on that night the luck of their spirit expired. Instead, the evil destructive forces of the devil, or *akuma*, were thrust upon them, in the form of a near typhoon strength storm, ominous in all respects.

By mid-1944 enemy ships were increasingly difficult to find. However, Intel reported moderate to busy ship traffic using the Luzon Strait between the Philippine and South China Sea. In July three boats, *Picuda*, *Spadefish*, and *Redfish* were sent as a Wolf-Pack to this area to investigate reports of enemy convoys in that general area. The weather was extreme; a storm raged and typhoon winds whipped the sea mad with spray and huge waves. Visibility was reduced to just a few yards. Search as they would the Wolf-Pack could not find the convoy. *Rasher*, commanded by Henry G. Munson, was patrolling in an adjacent area and word of the convoy reached them via radio.

At about 2000 hours on the 18th *Rasher* caught a brief glimpse of the convoy. The night was very dark but was illuminated by an occasional lightning flash. In one flash the captain saw the form of a large ship. The multiple targets and bad weather seemed to make obtaining a firing solution impossible but at just after 2100 hours he commenced firing a spread of four torpedoes from the stern tubes.[24] After two torpedoes were away the captain doubted the gyro settings so aborted the remaining two shots. However, those two torpedoes found their target with explosions that were both heard and seen by the *Rasher*. The captain believed he had struck a tanker because, as he wrote in his war patrol report, he believed the ship was:

...gasoline laden judging from the appalling explosion with a column of flame 1000 feet high. The entire sky was a bright red momentarily and the target and the whole convoy was seen for an instant. Part of the ship blew off and landed about 500 yards from the remainder of the tanker and both parts burned fiercely for about twenty minutes and then disappeared from sight in one final grand explosion.[25]

In the post-war years I worked with Commander Munson. We were teaching Electronics School at the Submarine School at New London. I knew him as a rather quiet type man, one of few words, and he definitely could not be called verbose. I am not surprised that his log entry, appearing later, describing his successful attack on what he thought was a gas-laden tanker was so brief. The Captain would not have been one to run on about it.

Rasher ended her war patrol with empty torpedo rooms and returned to Pearl Harbor and, eventually, to Hunter's Point Naval Shipyard in California for refit. They were informed on arrival that the tanker they thought they had sunk was actually the aircraft carrier *Taiyō,* that had sunk with over seven-hundred men and at least twenty-five aircraft.[26] At least one of *Rasher's* torpedoes had ruptured *Taiyō* avgas and oil tanks, causing them to explode giving the impression of a tanker carrying fuel. This was one of the most productive patrols of the war. According to reports compiled after *Rasher's* fifth war patrol she accounted for five ships sunk totaling over 57,700 tons, and four ships damaged totaling over 22,000 tons.[27]

When the submarine crewmen around the fleet heard the news of this aggressive and effective patrol the crew of the *Trout* could not help thinking that if we had had properly operating torpedoes during the early days of the war, might we have achieved similar results or, at least, not let "big ones' like the *Taiyō* get away? For this question only time will make it fade away without giving a clear answer. Our past disappointment aside, positive news about our torpedoes was greeted with enthusiasm. Two major defects were found and corrected in 1943: the contact exploder and the depth setting. Reliable torpedo performance would now be the norm.

CHAPTER 3

BATTLE SURFACE!

BY J. "DEEN" BROWN, RMCM(SS), USN(RET.)

Photo of the *Trout* (SS-202) underway on the surface
Author's Collection

MUCH HAS BEEN written about submarine torpedo attacks in World War II though not much has been published about submarine surface gun battles and the subsequent taking of P.O.W.s onboard. Some of my experiences while serving on the "Gold Sub", USS *Trout* (SS-202) are ascribed herein but the reader should be warned that the substance of this article is recalled from my faded memory and certain details may be inadvertently omitted. But that one order, ringing throughout the boat, is one-hundred percent clear in my memory: BATTLE STATIONS GUN ACTION! These words immediately strung our tensions high as we knew we would be engaging the enemy in their own waters, dangerously exposed to air and surface attacks. A lot of the crew heard BATTLE SURFACE and thought "God be with us"; our gun crews responded with "Give 'em Hell!" gusto and gave them their best.

My first experience with Japanese P.O.W.s was during the Battle of Midway. The IJN heavy cruiser *Mikuma* had been severely battered by our carrier aircraft. Being a tough, well-built ship, it stayed afloat but was derelict. *Trout* was vectored to its position and ordered to destroy it. Upon arrival, we found that the ship had sunk. A large field of debris and flotsam was all that remained of a once proud ship and its gallant sailormen warriors. As we threaded our way through the floating debris, we discovered two Japanese sailors clinging to a piece of the flotsam. We took them aboard and cleaned off a thick layer of black oil from them with juice and water. They were sunburned and dehydrated but quickly responded to kind treatment. One of these men was named Kenichi Ishikawa. He looked like a teenager but was actually twenty-one years old. He was quite happy to have been rescued but did not want to be returned to Japan because he feared being disowned by his family as a result of allowing himself to be captured alive and failing the Japanese Military samurai code. He talked freely about the makeup of the Japanese force that had been assembled to capture Midway Island. The older man, a man of about forty years, refused to talk. We thought he was upholding this code of honor and we figured we would leave the interrogation to the intelligence gurus at Pearl Harbor. We did learn that his name was Katsuichi Yoshida. When we got to Pearl, we turned them both over to the Marines. Sometime later Intelligence informed us that Mr. Yoshida was a Chief Radioman and was suffering in pain from seven broken ribs! No wonder he wouldn't talk; he was probably just biting back the pain. We were also told that these two were the first Japanese prisoners taken by our Navy following the declaration of war with Japan.

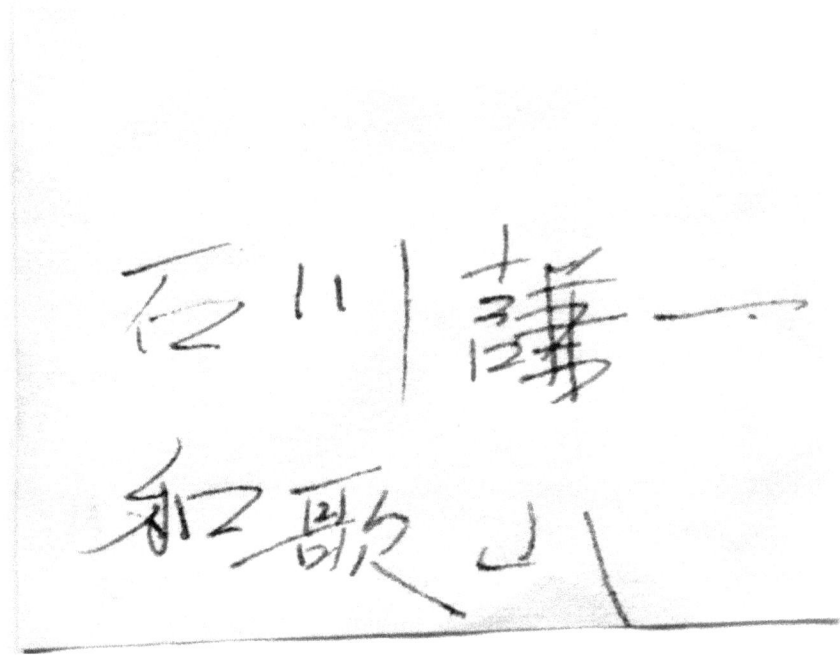

Japanese prisoners' names written in Japanese; Chief Radioman Hatsuichi Yoshida and Fireman 3rd Class Kenichi Ishikawa.
Author's Collection

Now a brief snap of the deck guns. The *Tambor* and *Gar* class boats were built with a three-inch gun mounted aft of the conning tower. Four thirty-caliber machine guns were also stowed onboard. The accuracy and the range of the deck gun was acceptable, but the three-inch projectile was too small and ineffective. Our crew dubbed it a "peashooter." After a few patrols from Fremantle, Australia, the peashooter was replaced with a much larger gun. The new gun was a "gem", a five-inch bore with a long barrel, I believe a 38 (38 times the bore of the barrel). The ammunition was semi-fixed (a casing held the powder), and the projectile was separate. A slight inconvenience compared to a single fixed ammo round.

The new gun gave the crew a welcome feeling of confidence. We could now inflict significant damage to a target at a longer range. Our original gun lost the confidence of the crew during the following battle.

We had attacked an enemy freighter in the Makassar Strait with torpedoes. Two of the torpedoes struck the ship blowing it into two pieces. The bow section, which was about a third of the ship, floated away. The aft section with the engine room was afloat. Torpedoes were scarce so Capt. Ramage chose not to spend another torpedo but sink it with our deck gun. For half an hour or more we pumped shells from the three-inch gun into the wreck. The captain decided to close range so we could more accurately strike the hull below the waterline and close we did. It was a logical plan but a bad call for us. The Japanese turned machine guns on us and racked the deck and gun crew with their fire. Seven of our crew were wounded and out of action with all having been struck in the legs. We were almost out of range, so the captain broke off the attack and turned away while we helped our wounded shipmates down the vertical ladder. When the deck was cleared, we submerged, and the captain elected to use a precious torpedo to finish off the ship; one torpedo sank her instantly.

We had several weeks to go on our patrol and our corpsman had a real challenge on his hands keeping the men's wounds from becoming infected in our unsanitary conditions onboard. Remember, penicillin was not readily available until much later in the war. After several weeks on patrol, we started back for Fremantle. The "Doc" had done his job well. Five of the wounded men were recovered and back to normal duty. The wounds of the remaining two men involved damage to their bones; one man's knee was badly shattered to the point where the leg had to be amputated and the other's heel had been hit and could not be fully restored. Both were medically discharged.

Two results came out of this incident. ComSubPac issued a directive that boats should remain out of range of enemy small arms fire and our crew welcomed the change to the more powerful five-inch gun they dubbed "Big Bertha" after a famed World War I gun. But as usual in such ordinance matters, there's always a flip side. We soon discovered the undesirable effects the big gun caused when fired. The recoil and concussion gave the after battery and engine room compartments a hefty shakeup. Furthermore, if the muzzle was lined over the superstructure, the concussion would blow the teakwood slats away. Though we wanted to keep it, it seemed like the gun was just a bit too much muscle for the *Tambor* class fleet boats.

Trout operated out of Fremantle for about two years. On each patrol we would surface and destroy small ships with the deck gun. Some were under sail and others were powered, but all were carrying supplies vital to Japan like precious metals, rubber, hemp, oil, and food and it was the submarine fleet's job to interdict this supply train. Often, these little ships' nationality was not displayed so our boarding parties would examine the cargo, ascertain their destination, and determine if the captain was Japanese. If the cargo was

AREA 18. PHILIPPINE ISLANDS - SULU ARCHIPELAGO - TAWI TAWI ISLANDS - SIBUTU ISLANDS -
SIBUTU ISLAND - SIBUTU PASSAGE. (App. Lat. 4° 50' N. - Long. 119° 40' E.) Gun attack
& burning of 2 Jap trawlers by USS Trout, 4-23-43, south Sibutu Passage. Periscope
setting --; lens opening, 22; shutter speed, 1/100; light conditions, bright; range,
inf.
ONI #175-164

Trout's (SS-202) handiwork - a burning Japanese trawler
Submarine Force Museum & Library Archives

war material, we would sink the craft with our gun. More than a few of these ships refused to stop when ordered, even when warning shots were fired across their bow. If so, we declared the ship and enemy and opened fire. Often the scene onboard caused by our gunfire was gruesome, a pure example of the horror of war. Some of our men would return from inspection nauseated; their upbringing had no preparation to cope with the terrible scenes of man's inhumanity to one another.

Early in a war patrol we intercepted a small freighter. Shots were fired across its bow and the ship came to an abrupt stop. Our boarding party found the cargo to be rubber. The captain and the chief engineer were both Japanese. The remainder of the crew were of mixed nationality: Korean, Filipino, and Vietnamese. Before sinking the ship we took the captain and the chief engineer prisoner and held the remaining men on deck. As we were only a few miles from land we gave these men a rubber raft and pointed them towards land. The last we saw of them they were paddling vigorously toward a nearby island.

The captain was an interesting fellow. He spoke English fluently and seemed calm and totally at ease with him captors. Later we learned that he had once lived in San Francisco and knew and

Trout captures Japanese lugger off the coast of Indo-China
Submarine Force Museum & Library Archives

understood Americans very well. This allowed him to be unaffected by the propaganda the Japanese government had spread that reported that if captured by the Americans, Japanese people would be slowly tortured and then murdered.

He volunteered to work while onboard, so he was made a mess cook; how ironic that he went from the command of a ship to the lowest position in just one day! He accepted his lot with dignity and toiled diligently at cleaning the cooking gear, washing the dishes, and scrubbing the galley and mess decks. He found enjoyment in our friendly relations and in our good food.

The Engineer was just the opposite. He seemed about thirty years old, and his gold front tooth let us know that he might have come from an aristocratic family. In Japan men of means often would have a perfectly good tooth removed and replaced with a gold one to make an obvious display of their wealth. This man was placed under guard in the After Torpedo Room and responded to his captivity my refusing food or drink. After several days of this we had his former Captain try to convince him that the Americans were not going to harm him and that he should end his fast. No avail; he refused to yield.

One day, after several weeks of this behavior, the guard called the Control Room to report that the prisoner was no longer moving. Sure enough, our Corpsman, with the Executive Officer, examined him and pronounced him dead. This occurred in the late afternoon. That night we were on the surface and had completed charging the batteries. The sea was very calm. We moved the Engineer through the Control Room, placed him in a gurney, and hoisted him up through the Conning Tower to the deck. A number of men and the remaining Japanese POW assembled and participated in a dignified burial ceremony befitting a man of the sea. With brief but proper honors the man's body was relinquished to the sea and passed beneath the waves.

Another surface event remains clear in my faded memory because of the pleasant and slightly comical nature of it. We stopped a fair-sized sailboat in the area of the Philippines that seemed too far out to be just fishing. As we approached, we recognized that the crew were all Filipinos and were terrified of us but when we identified ourselves as Americans they literally began to jump for joy! Captain Ramage had a crewmember that was of Philippine ethnicity to try to interrogate the fishermen to learn if they had seen any Japanese shipping. It was a good idea but one that failed because their dialect was unintelligible to our crewman.

As a friendly gesture we gave them food and water, both of which they accepted gladly. One of them knew a few English words and used them to ask for something that they desired very much: flour. Flour! One of our most basic staples and a gift that we would not have thought of ourselves, but this humble thing was like a gift from God to them! As evidence of the natural Filipino hospitality and their desire to repay our generosity they reciprocated with a gift to us: a chicken. One problem with this; the chicken was still alive! We had to graciously refuse and tried to explain that the chicken could not live on a submarine. We seemed to make our point without insulting them and we departed as friends, both crews waving their farewells.

We kept our big gun, but we had to return to the U.S.A. for a major overhaul. *Trout* had steamed all over the world for four long years after she was commissioned. Some of her machinery was badly worn and not dependable. Our route home was broken up by a stop in Pearl Harbor, Territory of Hawaii, where we moored alongside the USS *Scamp*. As I looked up at her bridge, I saw guns I had never seen before; they were 40 MM whereas ours were only 20 MM. I got more surprises when I looked down at *Scamp's* hull.

One area of the hull was so badly dished in that I thought that the indentation must have been stopped from going further and causing a hull rupture because it contacted a main diesel engine; and I was right! I wondered if those 40 MM guns could have contributed to this horrible damage, but I learned later that they had nothing to do with it.

From Pearl Harbor the *Trout* proceeded to the Hunter's Point Naval Shipyard at Mare Island, California. It was a long overhaul that kept us there until December of 1943. As the overhaul drew to an end, we all started wondering "When are they going to re-install Big Bertha?" The answer was not pleasing; Big Bertha was NOT going to be re-installed. Instead of our five-inch gun we would be getting a new four-inch, twenty-five caliber deck gun; for our gunners these words were a downer-downer. This short-barreled model would lack the range and accuracy to which we had become accustomed. Our very able XO, Lt. Harry Woodworth, tried to pin a happy face on the situation, as was his duty. Though the lieutenant was a highly respected officer, those battle-hardened, combat experienced gunners stood firmly by their convictions. Baptism under fire is a profound teaching experience! With reservations the gunners grudgingly accepted the unwelcome news that Big Bertha would not be coming back.

The new gun was soon dubbed the "Corn Popper" with more than a tinge of scorn. Purists may argue that these guns were meant for defensive purposes only. BUNK! The guns were there, we were at war, and wars are fought with all means available.

Trout departed San Francisco for Pearl Harbor in early 1944 after a week's delay due to a crewman's death from spinal meningitis that resulted in our quarantine. Once in Pearl we went through our pre-patrol training and then loaded the *Trout* for a prolonged war patrol, her eleventh. Our Chief Radioman had been hospitalized in Oakland, so he had not ridden the boat to Pearl, but a day prior to sailing he reported back aboard. That night I was told to pack my seabag; I would return stateside, on temporary orders, to attend school to study a new, advanced radar all the boats would soon be getting, and then return to the *Trout*. I was given the honor of casting off the No. 1 mooring line, the last line, all the while accepting the good-natured digs from my shipmates who called me landlubber, piker, and goldbricker to name a few. This was all in good fun, but it stung; I wasn't going to sea and to war with my crew and my boat.

That was the beginning of February. Around the end of the first week in April I was thinking that it was time for the *Trout* to end its patrol when I was summoned to the Squadron Office to receive the news; *Trout* wasn't coming home. Eighty-one of America's finest men and a legendary submarine were casualties of war. I was uncertain what would come next for me now that all of my friends and my floating home were gone.

The Squadron officer said that *Trout* was gone but *Gar* needs a radioman. He acknowledged my great loss but promised that if I could help out on *Gar* I would be transferred to the mainland to commission a new boat. I had made eight war patrols which, while being in no way near a record, was an impressive number, but I said yes without reservation; I think I was that eager for a new home.

Gar's mission was to provide air-rescue off the island of Peleliu during the invasion thereof. We rescued seven downed airmen during that battle. I must confess I was comforted knowing that we had our deck guns fully manned as we exposed ourselves to shore artillery fire.

As for the *Trout*, no one will ever know if her "Corn Popper" saw any use. That gun and any secrets will remain at the bottom of the China Sea forever.

Builders' plaque of the *Trout*. The plaque had been removed from the sub as she underwent repairs at Mare Island in late 1943 and was never reattached prior to her fateful 11th patrol.
http://www.navsource.org/archives/08/08202.htm
[accessed 3/6/2024]

CHAPTER 4

DARK IS THE HARBOR

BY J. "DEEN" BROWN, RMCM(SS), USN(RET.)

Deen Brown on USS *Trout* (SS-202), c. 1943;
Author's Collection.

IN THE EARLY years of World War II, the Japanese were aggressively carrying out their long-range military plan to control much of the land in the areas around the Japanese home islands and throughout the South Pacific. During years of planning and with acquisitions before the start of the global war, they came to the near realization of their plan to create the *Greater East Asia Co-Prosperity Sphere*. In the late 1930's they subdued and occupied coastal China and invaded Manchuria, the Dutch East Indies, Borneo and Sarawak, and other islands in that region. This was followed in 1941, by the onset of World War II and their invasion of the Philippine Islands; Singapore, Guam and Wake Island also fell before the wave of Japanese expansion. The people of Australia and New Zealand, countries on the periphery of Japan's grand plan, eyed this seemingly irresistible force with fear and apprehension.[28]

The result of Japan's execution of military conquest was thousands of prisoners of war, military and civilian alike, both from the United States and its allies. In the Philippines alone thousands of American military personnel were captured when that island nation fell. The Japanese found themselves ill-equipped to handle such a large number of prisoners; they lacked the facilities, supplies, and infrastructure to provide basic living requirements to sustain the influx of prisoners they had unexpectedly collected. As a result, in the time immediately following their capture, many of the fundamental requirements to support the life of the prisoners were ignored. Often, perhaps caused by the frustration at the lack of resources, the Japanese guards subjected their prisoners to brutal, inhumane treatment. This included but was not limited to deliberate starvation, denial of medicine, inadequate facilities for housing.[29]

After the war there were volumes written regarding the treatment that prisoners of war suffered at the hands of Japanese prison guards however, that information was not readily available during the war. When the perpetration of such human horror is taking place reports, hints, or rumors of what is going on begin to leak out. The occasional escaped prisoner, civilians who interacted with these prison camps and loose-lipped Japanese guards were all sources that fed the grapevine of information about what was going on inside these camps. This happened in much the same way that information regarding the Nazi Holocaust that began to filter its way into the public throughout the world. Once newspapers picked up these rumors and printed various snippets of information, this disturbing information filtered into the United States military units.

USS *Trout* (SS 202), c. 1943;
http://www.oneternalpatrol.com/uss-trout-202.htm

During the war I was stationed on the submarine, USS *Trout* (SS 202). Even on our boat, stationed in advanced areas, we started hearing about these prisoner of war camps and the kind of treatment and cruelty a prisoner could expect. Crew members talked about whether or not we would allow ourselves to be captured by the Japanese or choose some other more drastic option. There were many emphatic assertions made by my shipmates including some that said they would not allow themselves to be captured; whether or not they would have actually evaded capture by choosing that drastic alternative fortunately was never tested.

The Secretary of State, Cordell Hull, the Secretary of War, Henry L. Stimson, and President Roosevelt were very aware of the situation and knew too that the United States would have to lodge a protest with the Japanese to try and mitigate their terrible actions. One of the main problems that the government had was to find a credible and verifiable source of the information about the condition of the Japanese prisoner of war camps. In order to file a persuasive official protest, which would undoubtedly find its way into the news media and governments of both our allies and our enemies, the accusations had to be accurate, provable, and compelling. With these prerequisites in mind, government officials considered how to obtain very solid and irrefutable information about the treatment of these POW's held by the Japanese. Those requirements mandated that they needed to find prisoners of war who had escaped from those camps and get them back to the States where they could be interviewed. This was the task that they were faced with; very easy to describe but very difficult to accomplish.[30]

Since there had been such a large number of our personnel captured when the Philippines collapsed, much of the discussion centered on finding men who had escaped from prison camps in the Philippines that might provide vital, first-hand information. As luck would have it there was help to be had within the Japanese-controlled Philippine nation. After the takeover of the country, Philippine irregulars, sympathetic civilians, and free Allied military men who had evaded capture continued a guerilla war against the Japanese. These loosely organized forces had maintained radio contact with General MacArthur's staff located in Australia.

Through this resistance organization, intelligence was received that four United States military officers had escaped from the

Japanese prison camp system and were attempting to find some likely location for their evacuation from the islands. Considering the stranglehold the Japanese had on the land and airspace surrounding the Philippine nation, extraction by submarine seemed the only scenario likely to succeed. At the time, General Douglas MacArthur was responsible for the Allied war effort in the entire area of the South Pacific. As the senior officer in charge he was technically boss of all military forces operating in the South Pacific. However, he could not command use of a submarine since the Navy had arranged to retain operational control of their submarines. If the General's intelligence unit had a need for submarine services, such as running supplies, inserting coast watchers or, as in this case, rescuing personnel, they had to negotiate with the Navy officials for those services. Such was the case here; a slightly awkward system but one that ultimately achieved results.[31]

Once the Navy agreed to participate, the vital radio circuit between the Philippines guerillas and Douglas MacArthur's command center was activated and its security verified. Considerable intelligence information became available, the most relevant of which was passed on to the Navy. It became known that the escaped prisoners were on the Island of Mindanao; the rescue would have to be made from that island. The question that remained was when this extraction would be made. This seemingly simple question contained many factors that made it a very complex calculation. All aspects of the mission had to align favorably in order to carry out the rescue operation successfully and to do so without the loss of life or the loss of a submarine. One of the essential items was the time of day it would take place. It was decided that the rescue would be on a night of the new moon, no moon in the sky and therefore, no moonlight. This was a double-edged sword. The dark of the new moon would hide the submarine and its activities but it also rendered landmarks and nautical hazards near invisible. The other factor was mild weather. Unfortunately, since moonless nights occur in prescribed patterns, a meeting of both darkness and calmness would be dependent mostly on good luck.[32]

These important factors necessitated choosing an extraction area that was well charted so details were known about the shallow and potentially hazardous waters where our submarine would be entering. There were many things that had to be very carefully planned in advance in order to make this operation a success. One of them was close coordination so the plan, times of rendezvous, place and any changing factors could be transmitted to the prisoners via the Philippine guerrilla forces. This was essential to minimize the time that both the POWs and the submarine were exposed to the ubiquitous surveillance of the Japanese forces.

A great deal of planning took place before a final decision was made to send a submarine. This method of rescue received support from an unexpected civilian source. After the fall of the Philippines, one of our men captured was an Army Air Force Captain and a fighter pilot William E. Dyess. His father was a judge in Texas and was strongly convinced that a rescue of his son was feasible. Judge Dyess' letters carried a lot of weight since he was an important figure in Texas politics. He wrote his letters directly to President Roosevelt and General MacArthur requesting them specifically to send a submarine to rescue his son and any other prisoners of war that they could. Submarine extraction was popular to those with an interest in assuring the safety of these men due to the submarine's inherent advantage of stealth. Its very nature of invisibility and surprise exposed the sub and the men to be rescued to danger only for the shortest of time. Needless to say, though, both the sub and the escaped POWs had to make it through much danger and many hardships to arrive at that ultimate meeting.[33]

A harbor had to be selected on the island of Mindanao that would allow a submarine to get in close enough to the shore, so the escaping prisoners had the shortest distance to travel; the harbor in Davao Gulf was chosen. Davao Gulf is a large gulf on the southern tip of Mindanao that was quite well-known, had up-to-date maritime charts readily available, and had a Japanese prisoner of war camp located there; it was even possible that these prisoners may have escaped from that particular camp. Planning and detailed analysis of that body of water, the land, the weather predictions at that location, at that time of year were very carefully examined.

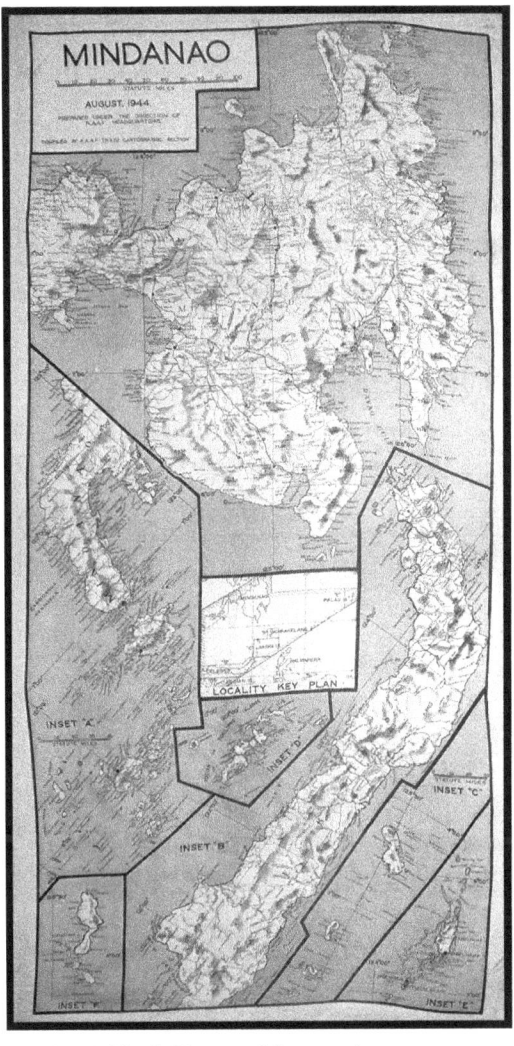

RAAF Cloth Escape Map, c. August 1944
http://www.escape-maps.com/escape_maps/wwii_raaf_mindanao.htm

Once it was decided to use a submarine the question remained, which submarine to choose? After looking at the various available submarines, the choice became quite obvious. There was one submarine that had been into the Philippines a number of times, had performed operations and a number of special missions there, and was quite familiar navigating in the Philippine waters; it was the USS *Trout* (SS-202).

Trout had made a name for herself by entering Manila Bay prior to the fall of the Philippines. Right under the nose of the Japanese the crew loaded the boat with over twenty tons of gold and silver, bearer bonds, currency, and paper money. At the same time as the crew was loading the sub, Corregidor was being incessantly bombed by the Japanese. This cargo was effectively the valuable contents of the Philippine treasury and the United States embassy. This treasure was removed by the "Gold Sub" and safely delivered to Pearl Harbor from where it was transshipped to the United States mainland for safe keeping. That they managed to pull off this economic extraction made quite a name for the boat and crew in the Pacific submarine force.[34]

Trout got orders to depart. In addition to bringing back the escaped POWs, the *Trout* would take this opportunity to land supplies for the local resistance and to put ashore a group of twenty U. S. Army Special Forces. They were to join up with the Filipino Scouts and the other Philippine underground groups to lead, guide, and help continue the effort to battle the Japanese Army in the Philippines. The Special Forces men came aboard with a large cache of supplies that included such things as ammunition, medicine, and batteries. As a Radioman, I could see that some types of batteries were obviously intended for a radio-set use. We knew that the Philippine underground had radio operations and they had an active radio circuit between the Philippines, McArthur, and Australia, so a re-supply of batteries seemed an essential item.

Among the other different things that were in this cache of supplies was an array of so-called booby traps. We didn't like those! The Special Forces fellows told us that some of those things were

At Pearl Harbor in early March 1942, unloading gold bars which had been evacuated from Corregidor.
https://www.history.navy.mil/content/history/nhhc/our-collections/ photography/numerical-list-of-images/nara-series/80-g/80-G-40000/80-G-45971.html

designed to either injure or kill an enemy if they picked one up or even moved it. One of the bombs was fabricated in the form of an old-fashioned Brownie box camera that contained enough explosives to kill half a dozen or so people that might be in close proximity. Another looked like a man's wallet. If someone picked it up, it would blow their hands off and perhaps they would bleed to death unless they were able to get help. These so-called booby traps were useful for them but we were uncomfortable having such things in our fragile submarine. I estimate that we had close to a ton of that material to get onboard; we handled it very gently and didn't have to tell people more than once why such care was needed. That was our cargo.

Eventually, we managed to get on our way and headed on our mission to the Philippines on 27 May 1943. Our orders were:

WHEN DIRECTED ABOUT 28 MAY PROCEED VIA LOMBOCK AND MAKASSAR STRAITS TO THE VICINITY TO. MANGKALIHAT AND PATROL THAT AREA FOR A PERIOD OF ABOUT 6 DAYS. THENCE PROCEED TO SOUTH COAST MINDANAO TO ARRIVE NOT EARLIER THAN 11 JUNE AND EXECUTE SPECIAL MISSION.[35]

The *Trout* travelled through the Indian Ocean to the Lombok Passage and the Makassar Strait into the seas in and around the Philippines. The Indian Ocean is very large and open and it can be very rough. After we were underway for about a day, one of our crew members rather jokingly asked one of the Special Forces guys, "Well, what do you think of your first submarine ride?" He looked at him disgustingly and said, "If you're going to stop, I'll get off anywhere!" More than a few of them were seasick and very uncomfortable but they all managed all right and they all survived their first sub ride.

Other than that our voyage to the Philippine area was uneventful. The Captain did not want to risk being spotted because the plan was to go undetected in as far as we possibly could. Therefore, we travelled on the surface only at night and stayed submerged during daylight hours.

We got along very well that way but deviated from our plan once to attack a Japanese merchant ship around dawn on June 9th. We fired three torpedoes from the stern tubes but, as the captain noted, that ship was, "scared but undamaged."[36] The *Trout* arrived off of Mindanao a little ahead of schedule which was good because our navigators had to study Davao Bay in detail; navigating into that bay in the darkness of a moonless night without lights was going to be a challenge to be sure. The bay is rather large; its expanse stretches for several miles. Because of its size and the distance of the far shores, our captain decided that we could travel on the surface into the bay using our normal diesel engines for quite a distance but towards the head of the bay we secured the diesel engines in order not to make noise. The diesel engines were quite loud and their sounds could easily be detected on shore or by a patrol craft in the bay itself. We proceeded the rest of the way on silent battery power alone.

In the darkness of the night on June 11th, it was impossible for the navigators to use landmarks for checking our position in the harbor. The only thing we could go on was an estimate based on radar data but that data was 'broad' and not precise enough to pinpoint our position. The reality was navigating into that bay and into the harbor on that dark night was a 'feel-as-you-go' proposition. Additionally, there were any number of possible problems that we could get ourselves into not the least of which was running aground. We never knew exactly whether we were in a shipping channel or out of it so even knowing that there were underwater objects to be avoided was not that helpful since we were unsure exactly where <u>we</u> were![37]

At any rate, in the interest of safety to the ship, the captain decided that we would open the ballast tank vent valves and flood down the boat to where the decks were just about awash. We retracted all the devices that extended below the keel, such as the sonar sensors, so there would be nothing protruding to strike the bottom. The wisdom of these two precautionary measures was that if we should run aground we could blow air into the partially-flooded ballast tanks, lift ourselves up, and get ourselves off of whatever might have hung us up. Fortunately, we proceeded very, very, slowly and cautiously, and no problems occurred.

We finally arrived at our destination a mile or so from the shore and the city of Davao. Close to the shore there were no currents that we could detect so we didn't worry much about drifting, although

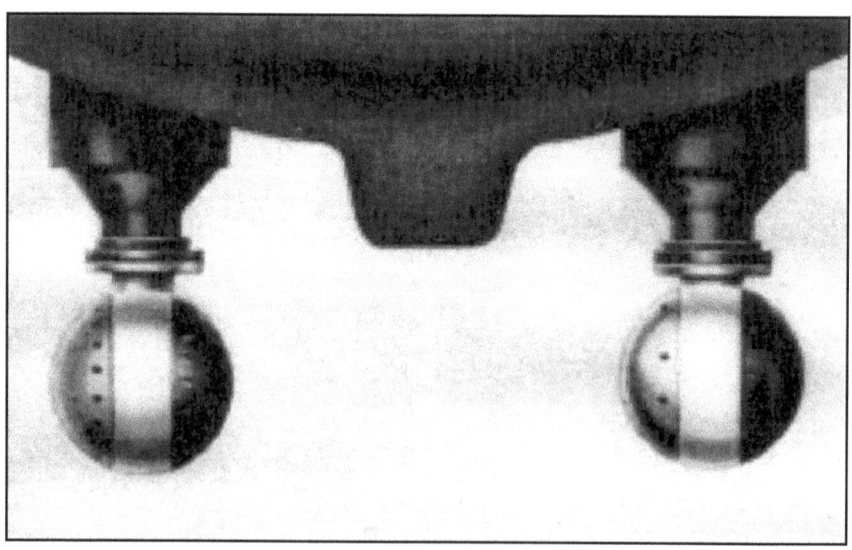

"The Two Hydrophones (Projectors) are mounted at the bottom of shafts, which extend through the hull under the forward torpedo room. Lowering these shafts puts the two projectors below the keel."
From *http://maritime.org/doc/fleetsub/sonar/chap1.htm#1A*

we still had to be cognizant of that and we remained in place where we had stopped. As difficult as sneaking into the harbor had been, that was the easy part. Now came the hard part: waiting for the passengers to come to us. We'd gone in as far as we could go so there was nothing more that we could do except station lookouts, watch for any sign of any activity on the shore, and wait. Since the sonar heads were retracted all that was available to us to listen for approaching enemy patrol craft were the eyes and ears of the crew; many eyes that peered into darkness to detect any sign of activity and, many ears that strained to hear the noise of a nearby vessel.

The Captain ordered the crew members that were not on duty, or on watch down below, to come up on deck about fifteen or twenty at a time. We were evenly positioned all the way from the bow to the stern and given the first overriding instruction; do not talk. We were so close to the land and it was so quiet that even a man's voice might be heard onshore. Only if we had something to report were we allowed to talk and that could only be delivered in a whisper. Though the situation, the danger, and the excitement may have warranted it, yelling out or calling a loud report, no matter how vital, was absolutely forbidden. Also, no one was allowed to carry anything up on deck that might drop and make a noise.

We expected and looked for some sort of a light, a signal light, which would flash to us and hopefully give us a proper identification signal that had been prearranged before our arrival. We could see campfires on the beach about a mile or so from us; presumably in the local people's camps. The fires offered us a bit of a distraction and also made us aware that there were other human beings near.

It was the early hours when we established our lookout and we remained in that position for quite a while waiting and watching and listening. Waiting in a situation like that was torturous; the stress due to of the possibility of attack with no warning wore the crew out. The ever-present danger of being detected stretched the minutes into hours. As bad as it was for the vigilant crew, it was worse for the captain since he was ultimately responsible for the boat, the crew, and the freedom of the POWs and Captain Clark showed some signs of stress. He did not normally smoke, but while he was topside slowly pacing the deck, watching everybody, and peering out into the darkness, he had a cigar clamped between his teeth. He never lit it; it was just something for him to chomp on during this seemingly endless period of waiting.

I was up on the deck taking my turn with my shipmates. I was positioned just about parallel to our conning tower which was just about amidships. I kept looking at the fires on the beach and wondering about them. I could smell smoke from the fires and it seemed extremely strong. I believed the odor of the wood smoke was much too strong to be coming from these distant campfires. The captain was close by so I whispered my thoughts about the smoke smell to him. He naturally was a bit on edge, but he turned and looked at me as if I had lost my mind. He whispered back, "Well, of course! Can't you see those fires burning over there in the beach?" Well, yes, I could see them, that didn't put me at ease. In my hometown of Schell City, in western Missouri, I had spent many nights around a campfire on the Osage River fishing for catfish, blue cats, and channel cats. I knew quite well how strong a campfire odor is especially when one is really close to it. That's what toggled my mind, got me excited about it; that smoke odor just seemed unnaturally strong.

Not wanting to further distract the captain, I didn't say any more about it. The question became moot anyway because one of our lookouts had spotted what appeared to be a very dim light in the darkness of the shore. We expected that we'd probably see nothing any brighter than a small flashlight and that was just what this tiny light looked like. Our signalman was standing by on the deck with a battery powered Aldis Lamp, a signaling device. It was made so that you had to be directly in front of it or you could not see the light; it was shaped somewhat like an oversized shotgun.

We kept staring into the darkness, at the place the light had first been seen and sure enough, it appeared again. Our signalman read a recognition signal, and he replied with the Aldis lamp; his sign was acknowledged. Bravo! We had made contact! Since we were in as close as we could get, we waited for them to travel the distance out to

Portable Aldis Lamp
(without light shield)
https://www.liverpoolmuseums.org.
uk/maritime-museum
[accessed 3/8/2024];
Public Domain Image

the *Trout*, which had closed to maybe a half of mile or so. We had sighted the recognition signal and received the correct recognition code but still it was time to wait some more; it seemed excruciating, waiting just those few more minutes. I'm sure it was just a few minutes but whatever it was, we certainly experienced a long, long wait! Everyone was on edge and eagerly waiting to see our passengers but we didn't know what to look for precisely. We didn't know whether those men would have a rubber raft, whether they'd have a rowboat, perhaps kayaks or just paddle out holding something. We kept straining, looking for something, anything!

After about ten minutes, there began to appear in the darkness a startling sight; it looked like the bow of a large ship. We were expecting to see a small vessel so the size of this ship's bow shocked us. Were we going to be rammed? Had we been discovered by the Japanese? As it came closer and as the illusion of the dark night begin to fade away, we could see more plainly that it wasn't such a large ship, just a boat of moderate size. It finally came close enough so that it could see us and in very seaman-like manner, the boat turned and headed its bow in the same direction as our bow and moved alongside. We very quickly threw a mooring line over and the Filipino sailors greeted us; that was really a very, very big relief to all of us on the *Trout*. Finally, they were securely moored alongside.

There were three men onboard that appeared to be passengers who were dressed a little differently than the Filipino crewmen. We couldn't see them too well in the dark, but soon they were getting ready to come aboard. They were helped aboard and immediately escorted to a hatch to go below decks. Our captain stopped them and said, "I was told there were four of you. Where is the fourth man?" One of them replied, "Sam is not here. He did not come," and they kept on going to get below decks. We learned later that the Sam he mentioned was in fact Lieutenant Samuel C. Grashio, U. S. Army Air Corp. He had decided to remain in the Philippines to join up with the freedom fighters to assist in getting them organized, supplied, and fighting the Japanese military; that's why we ended up with three passengers instead of four.[38]

The captain was anxious to get out of there and get underway. His cigar was getting shorter and shorter! He asked the captain of the boat to move so we could get underway. It turned out that the boat the Filipinos had was in fact a small tug; we were very surprised that they would have a boat of that size. One of our crewmen asked one of the Filipinos, "How did you get that tug?" The crewman looked at him rather casually and said, "Oh, we just go aboard and take it," and said no more. In plain sight was a bolo knife hanging from his belt. It was probably anywhere from twelve to eighteen inches in length. I then looked around at the other Philippine crewmen and they all had bolo knives. Based on what I knew of the Filipino freedom fighters, it was plain what he meant when they told us that, "We just go aboard and take it." I did not need a scene painted for me; that was enough. I was glad they were on <u>our</u> side!

While the tug laid alongside I noticed that I didn't hear any engines running; it was very quiet. I noticed also that there was smoke coming from a smoke stack in this small boat so I assumed the tug was steam powered, and that's why I didn't hear a noise. Out of curiosity I asked one of the crewmen what they were using for fuel. He said, "Oh, we're burning coconut husks." In other words, that tug was powered by an old fashioned wood-burning steam engine. Old fashioned, but it did the job that day. When I learned that the tug was a wood-burner, I knew that it was responsible for that heavy smoke smell I had earlier reported to the captain.

Our captain signaled that we were getting underway and that final preparations should be made and the tug should cast off. The deck of the *Trout* all of a sudden got incredibly busy. Our Special Forces passengers began disembarking onto the tug and had the help of many of our crew to pass over their useful and dangerous cargo. As men and material flowed onto the tug one more passenger came onto the *Trout*, almost unobserved. He was Commander Charles "Chick" Parsons, U. S. Navy. CDR Parsons had been landed in the Philippines where he located and worked with General (formerly Colonel) Wendell Fertig, the self-appointed commander of the Philippine resistance forces. Fertig was very effective in providing an organizational focus for the patchwork of isolated and escaped Allied forces, free Philippine military, and post-occupation volunteers. His ad hoc command structure was aided by people like

Parsons who helped obtain and direct vital supplies where they were needed most while avoiding detection by the Japanese. *Trout* would ferry Parsons to another island where he would disembark and continue his mission. We had had Parsons as a passenger on *Trout* several times before on these island-hopping missions.[39]

Colonel Fertig wearing red goatee during the war. *Public Domain Image.*

Just as the flow from *Trout* to the tug ended, one of the tug's crewmen jumped up and said, "Wait, wait, wait, wait!" Quickly, he and the rest of the crew started grabbing wicker baskets and passing them up to us, baskets filled with different kinds of wild fruit from the local area. While waiting for the rendezvous, these men had collected baskets of fruit like papayas and breadfruit, along with several stalks of bananas, to give to us during the transfer of the escaped POWs. This action was in keeping with their well-known hospitality but this time they really hit the mark. Getting fresh fruit and vegetables on a submarine was like finding a gold mine; the sub crew was delighted to get these treats.

We very quickly and just as quietly loaded this fresh bounty, cast off the tug, and turned to start out of the harbor, again using battery power. As we left our Filipino freedom fighters we silently waved our thanks and goodbyes until they disappeared into the darkness; we had made new friends! The topside lookouts made their way below. We traveled for quite a distance on battery power because, again, we did not want to make noise with the diesel engines. After perhaps half an hour or so on battery power, we concluded that we were far enough away from the concentrations of Japanese military that we could risk starting the engines, which we did, and the engines roared to life. Their deafening noise was somehow relaxing after the hours of tense silence we had just experienced. We blew our ballast tanks high and dry and sped off for the open sea.

Below decks, the crew was busy unloading the baskets of fruit and vegetables and putting them in their proper place. While this was happening our chief cook decided that the prisoners must be hungry and they would probably like to have food and water and maybe something special. He went to our freezer where he carefully selected three big choice-looking steaks to be ready to be cooked for these deprived and hungry men. Before the cooking began he went to the wardroom where the passengers were and asked them if they had any particular food request of something we might have onboard. The cook was ready to surprise them with the idea of the juicy steaks but, instead, he was met with silence. Finally one of them spoke up and said, "Sir, if you have any milk aboard, could we possibly have some milk and bread?"

A deflated and humbled cook came back to the galley area in the mess hall, where most of our crew was waiting. He announced to us, "Guess what? They don't want steaks. They want bread and milk!" Our milk was powdered and it took him a while to prepare that since, to improve its flavor, it was chilled with some ice. Our bread was baked on board and fortunately we had an excellent baker so we had very good baked products to offer these former prisoners.

That reply from the prisoners, because it was such a humble request, sobered us and tempered our youthful exuberance. There were quite a few crew members who were in the States during the Great Depression when it was common for some people, especially in rural areas, to have bread and milk as their staple diet; I remembered those times myself. Cornbread was eaten during the week but on Sunday they might have what was called "white bread," a treat, though some called it light bread. The prisoner's request for this most modest meal made us think solemnly about how fortunate we were.

After our new passengers had an opportunity to have some food, something to drink, they were invited to take a shower even though our submarine had a very meager supply of fresh water. Normally the crewmen could not take showers, except when in port, so this was a luxurious offer. They all accepted and began to look more refreshed. During this clean-up some of the crew members gathered clothing and offered it to these men so they could wear some fresh, clean clothes.

One of the first priorities was for our hospital corpsman or 'Doc', as we called him, to examine them, in particular to see if there were signs of parasites. One of the things that was very troubling to people in close confinement like in a submarine was body lice or, as we called them, 'crabs'. Doc examined their hair very carefully and treated each one with a medicated powder. In the enclosed environment of a submarine, if one man should have body parasite of any type, they can quickly multiply, and soon inhabit every man onboard if they're not very quickly eradicated.

Another major concern of the Doc was the large sores which covered the lower legs and forearms of these three men. These sores were caused by bee stings, insect and jungle leech bites. The leeches would attach themselves to any bit of exposed skin, bite in, and feed on the man's blood. These men knew they were not supposed to pull the leeches off forcefully, but some had done so anyway, probably because the sight of those creatures attached to your body feeding on your blood was just too revolting! When a leech was removed by force they often left behind mouth-parts in the wound that caused infection to occur. Having no medicine, the men had self-treated these wounds with poultices of chewed tobacco and it seemed to help a bit. Doc traded this remedy for more modern medicine and was able to clear up these sores in a matter of days.[40]

Most of the crew members on board, including myself, knew little or nothing about these three men. For myself, I understood that our captain knew their names since they had been supplied to him prior to our departure from Australia. I enticed our yeoman to write their names and ranks on a piece of paper, and post it on a small bulletin board in the mess room so we could properly address them with courtesy and respect. The senior officer of the three was Major Stephen M. Mellnik, U. S. Army. He was a member of the Coast Artillery Corps. There was also a Navy officer, Lieutenant Commander Melvin H. McCoy. He had been assigned in the Philippine area was captured along with many others when Corregidor fell. Finally, there was Captain William E. Dyess. He was U. S. Army Air Corps, and a fighter pilot in the Philippine area. These officers had worked and planned long and hard to escape from the prison camp, and managed to survive in a jungle environment with the help, at times, from some Filipino personnel; very often, though, they traveled alone. They were very persistent and refused to give up even through their hardship, which was why they now found themselves safely aboard the *Trout*.[41]

All three men were very gaunt. They were in good spirits, and of course very pleased to be aboard but there were clear signs they had suffered greatly from lack of food, the harsh conditions in the jungle, and the stress of constant pursuit. Major Mellnik was very quiet and not a big man; if he had been, he'd lost so much of his weight that he was a rather small fellow by the time we met him. He had a very prominent scar on his face. We found out later that

Major (former Capt.)
William E. Dyess
Public Domain Photo;
The Dyess Story,
G.P. Putnam's Sons, 1944

a Japanese officer had attempted to behead him with his sword for some supposed offense. Mellnik ducked when the Japanese swung at him and the sword struck him across the face. It left a red and angry scar but the major managed to keep his head; that spared his life.

Lieutenant Commander McCoy was also very underweight but, other than that, he looked and acted quite normal. He was usually in good spirits, had fairly good health, and looked young mostly due to his dark, almost black hair. Some of the Filipinos apparently trimmed his hair before he came aboard; this good grooming only added to his pleasant and healthful appearance.

Captain William Dyess was the youngest of the three and that was to his benefit. He was energetic and seemed to enjoy visiting and talking to us. He was quite interested in the operations of the submarine and questioned us about what individual components did and what made them 'tick.' It was not unlike him to ask, "Hey Deen, what does this valve do?" or a number of other similar questions. He was obviously technically minded and was intrigued by the workings of our boat. That was generally their demeanor when they first came aboard. These three men, each in their own way, were very pleasant companions and welcome additions to our happy crew and we went out of our way to be courteous and pleasant to them.

Our "Special Mission" took two days to accomplish, June 11th and 12th. On the morning of the second day, after our passengers were safely aboard, the captain dove at dawn and conducted a submerged patrol in Moro Gulf to give the crew a, "much deserved rest after two busy nights."[42] In the days following our departure from Davao Gulf, we proceeded southward and eventually headed back to Australia. Near dawn on June 15th, the sonar had detected a ship, a large ship. After observation the captain recognized the ship as a tanker and began tracking the ship to get in a firing position. The *Trout* was put through her paces to get into position; it was not until almost noon that the captain began his approach. The ship initially appeared unescorted, traveling alone at a rather leisurely speed, but at 1210 an escort ship joined the tanker. Thirty-two minutes later three torpedoes left their tubes and headed towards the tanker at a range of 1450 yards. The fire control man who helped operate the torpedo data computer stood with his stopwatch in hand timing the run of the torpedoes. He knew exactly how long it should take to intersect the target. And intersect it did! Suddenly there was a very large explosion as the first torpedo decimated the after third of that ship. The second fish, "eliminated the whole after half." The third torpedo struck as well and, "left only bow and foremast floating." The captain later noted that, concerning this attack, "No description of hits possible except to say whole sections completely disappeared instantaneously with terrific explosion."[43]

The escort worked away and eventually dropped a few depth charges but at quite a distance from us. The captain looked through the periscope and decided that is was safe enough that the passengers could have a look at our handiwork. He invited the passengers to come to the conning tower and to view the remainder of the stricken tanker. They came up one by one, Major Mellnik first. He looked through the periscope for a few seconds, turned to the captain and said, "Well, that ship is done," and then went on his way.

The next was Lt. Col. McCoy who looked for about ten seconds and noted that there were survivors in the water who apparently had time to abandon their ship. He folded the handles up on the periscope, and said to the Captain like, "Well, they won't bother anyone anymore," and then went on his way.

A Japanese ship sinking, seen from USS *Seawolf's* periscope,
as the result of torpedo attack, fall 1942; ship was possibly Gifu Maru,
sunk in Davao Gulf, Philippine Islands, 2 Nov 1942
[typical post-attack periscope sighting].
Public domain image

It was then Captain Dyess's turn. He looked through the periscope for quite a long while, maybe half a minute. Finally he turned to the captain and said, "Captain Clark, do you have a carbine on board? If you do, if you'll give it to me and take me up there, I'll kill every one of those bastards." Captain Clark looked at him very soberly, straight in the eye and said, "Captain Dyess, we don't do that." So that was that. It was obvious that Captain Dyess wanted some payback for the gruesome and inhuman suffering that he had gone through, he and many, many more like him. We could certainly understand his feeling, but Captain Clark was right; "We don't do that."

The rest of the ship sank by 1440 and the escort never gained our contact. Running on batteries we held our own in the current until about 1900 when we surfaced and resumed our way to Australia on all engines. While cruising enroute to Australia which took us several days, there was not much activity on the ship. We did encounter some schooners on the 19th and almost shot them up but instead decided to interrogate them. Good decision! These were local boats with credentials from the U. S. – Philippines Army to haul foodstuff to support the freedom fighters on Mindanao.[44]

The passengers spent some of their time just meandering through the ship, talking to the crewmen about things on the submarine and sometimes just small talk that didn't involve the submarine at all; it seemed they enjoyed just chatting with us. I was often on duty in the radio room. They would stop by and if I could spare some time without wearing my headphones, I would talk with them and explain a few things that were going on in electronics. Commander McCoy was very interested in the sensors that we had onboard. I could tell from his questions that he had been involved with some type of data collection or the employment of tactical sensors. He was very interested in our radars. I explained to him that we had two; one was for aircraft detection only, not for sea-surface detection. It would give us some information, but not all that we could have used. For an example, it would tell us that there was an aircraft up there, how far off the aircraft was, that is the range, but would not give us azimuth; we didn't know the direction of the aircraft. That sounds bad but the direction of an airplane was not very important to us. What was most important is that we know there was one up there that might do us harm so we could dive and avoid being sighted.

He was also intrigued about our other radar. I explained to him that we had a tactics and navigation radar which would give us contacts on anything on the surface of the sea, including land, ships, or any other object, especially if it was metallic. I told him that particular radar was operating at a very high frequency, at a wavelength of about ten centimeters. He was surprised to learn that we had equipment on board that would operate at such a high frequency. McCoy told me that his last duty station was aboard the cruiser, the USS *Marblehead*. The highest frequency equipment they had on-board was something on the order of 50 MHz (megahertz), which in those days was called megacycles.

At any rate he was very interested in this centimeter radar. I did not pursue that conversation with him because details about this radar were highly classified. The generation of energy at that wavelength in the UHF (ultra-high frequency) region or centimeter-wavelength region, and the components used to generate such frequencies were classified SECRET. We radiomen who had been to school to study radar were instructed to never mention the name of the component that would generate such a short wavelength. That component, a unique vacuum tube, was obtained by the United States from Great Britain. It was developed in England by British physicists and was called a 'cavity magnetron.' I was not allowed to repeat those words aloud, speak it in any conversation, or mention it to anyone. Although I would not discuss the secret components with Commander McCoy, there were a considerable number of other things that we were able to talk about. He was quite an interesting fellow who was fascinated by the same things that I was.[45]

The U.S. Navy light cruiser USS *Marblehead* (CL 12)
underway at sea, 10 May 1944. *Public Domain Image;*
https://www.history.navy.mil/our-collections/photography/numerical-
list-of-images/nhhc-series/nh-series/NH-98000/NH-98035.html
[accessed 2/29/2024].

Commander McCoy remarked to me that he had some experi-ence onboard the *Marblehead* in communications, but he had not revealed this to his Japanese interrogators. Good thing as it turned out. I found out many later in years that Commander McCoy was, in fact, a cryptanalyst, i.e. a code-breaker. He was stationed in a cryp-tographic intelligence team just prior to the loss of the Philippines. Had he admitted that to his captors his lifespan would not have lasted thirty seconds. He was withholding his secrets from me as I was from him, but I didn't know that at the time. I also later learned that Commander McCoy wanted very much to return to the Pacific war zone. After a period of recuperation he requested to return to duty in the war-zone but the Navy would not allow it. With the sensitive information he had they simply could not take another chance on him being captured by the Japanese, interrogated a second time, and perhaps not being able to withhold his secret information. So, he was not allowed to go back to a war zone.[46]

McCoy and Dyess both were eager for news of home and the war and if one of my shortwave sets were free they would put on some headphones and search around the dial for a clear station broadcasting in English. Sometimes they would find one and soak up as much news as they could until the signal faded. One evening Capt. Dyess was on the headphones when he jumped up, threw them down and began ripping off a string of obscenities that I would have previously believed could only come from a white-hat sailor. As he got a little calmer I finally made out the words, "Tokyo Rose," amidst the swearing. Once he was in a mood for listening I told him that we didn't really pay any attention to the constant stream of propaganda that came from that Japanese gal. However, I think I understood. To us, she was a entertainment and her propaganda claims were absurdly humorous. Dyess's prison camp experience had no humor in it so Rose's theatrically mocking voice generated anger, not humor. He recovered soon enough though, and was a good shipmate throughout our short journey back to Australia.

While it was mostly calm on our way back we did have some opportunity to strike at our enemy. On June 26th the *Trout* encountered three steam coasters and engaged them in a surface gun action. Using 20 mm gunfire and shells from our 3" gun, all three of these Japanese supply vessels, 1200 tons total, were sunk. Additionally, on July 1st we encountered several patrol boats and a marked hospital ship near Verde Island Passage. We avoided these ships but managed to find a large tanker at 0344 on the morning of July 2nd. The captain easily put us in position and fired four bow torpedoes. At 0405 the first torpedo blew the bow clean of that tanker and a minute later the forth torpedo made it a certainty. By 0430 the tanker was gone from the sea.[47]

On July 20th, prior to our arrival in Australia, we received a radio message instructing us to rendezvous with a small boat at a distance of about ten miles from the Fremantle Harbor in Western Australia. We didn't know what that was all about but we assumed that perhaps some officials might come out and board us. At any rate, when we finally got to our rendezvous point the small boat was there. They came alongside and transferred some boxes of material to us and then left. We took them and put them down below before we could find out what we were actually handling.[48]

It turned out that the boxes contained clothing. The Army Staff in Western Australia had arranged to have a dress uniform for each of the Army officers and a Navy uniform for Commander McCoy. We were due to arrive in just a few hours alongside the quay in Fremantle Harbor and apparently there would be press and cameras there and the officials wanted the prisoners to be appropriately dressed for that occasion. The former POWs changed into their uniforms and were ready to disembark. When we arrived at the quay in Fremantle they were met by high ranking Army and Navy officers. Our passengers formed abreast and marched into two waiting staff cars.

Quite a few of the *Trout's* crew were on deck and we watched them as they headed for the staff cars. As they marched in a military manner towards the cars they appeared to be happy and very proud. They had gone through a tremendous life-changing ordeal and come out safely. Now they were once again free American fighting men back in their military organization, and ready to continue the fight. It seemed to me that they tried to communicate this feeling by their attempts at correct "military bearing." However, even though they tried to march and stand erect with heads held high, their bodies had been affected by torture, privation, and exertion. Their attempts, though, almost said more than they could have; a faltering step or crooked back told of how much this freedom had cost. We watched them until they finally got in the car and disappeared. Our friends for a brief time, dressed in their ill-fitting uniforms, were gone.

The departure of our passengers was the end of a unique period for us on *Trout*. It was now time to resume our normal duties and prepare the boat for turnover to the Relief Crew. They took charge of the *Trout*, stood our watches, corrected all deficiencies, replenished all supplies, and generally made the boat ready for her next war patrol. We got two weeks off to rest and recreate at a local resort that the Navy procured for returning submarine crews. As usual, I and my shipmates enjoyed the opportunity to relax and replenish our own diminished supplies but even as we had our fun the question in our minds was, "Where will we go next?" Would it be to the waters around the Philippines again or to Java, Okinawa, or even the Sea of Japan? We didn't have an answer but an answer was blowing-in-the-wind; as it turned out, our next patrol would be different but successful like the previous one. On her tenth war patrol *Trout* would be credited with the sinking of a trawler, a troop transport, a merchant-*maru*, and an *I-62* class submarine for a total of over 15,000 tons. However, as we waited for this patrol we really wanted most to know how our late passengers and new friends were faring. Unfortunately, this information would not be available to us until after the end of the war. Like the many islands we passed and the shipmates we had known these three men, for us, had simply disappeared.[49]

Though they disappeared for us, these three men made a significant impact on the conditions inside the Japanese military prison system. Not long after his return to the States Captain Dyess provided a complete account of his experiences as a POW. This report, and the reports of the other escapees, were forwarded to the War Department, the State Department, and ultimately to the President. The dilemma they had was judging whether the release of this information would improve the treatment of prisoners or bring retribution down upon them. In early December, 1943, the President ordered Dyess's report to be temporarily squelched. General MacArthur objected immediately to this directive stating that other Allies, like the Australians, already knew of the camp atrocities, and were moving forward with their own measures. When his objection was dismissed and the directive was reaffirmed, the General, not surprisingly, took matters into his own hands. He contacted the Philippine territorial commander, Japanese Field Marshal Hisaichi Tersuchi, and informed him that he, MacArthur, would hold Japanese commanders personally responsible for, "any failure to accord the prisoners proper treatment." His message had the desired effect. In late December the Japanese chief of the Prisoner of War Bureau issue a warning to all camp commanders. "Care should be taken to avoid issuing twisted reports of our fair attitude which might give the enemy food for evil propaganda and bring harm to our interned brothers," the message stated, undeniably a diplomatic way of saying, "The jig is up. Stop abusing your prisoners."[50]

Following this, the State Department became aware that Red Cross supplies, previous being withheld or diverted for Japanese use, began making their way into the hands of the POWs. Seeing that the information about camp conditions was already leaking out and it was causing conditions to improve, the Dyess information was finally released to the American press followed promptly by press releases from the State Department based on reports from Dyess, Mellnik, and McCoy. Secretary of State Hull, now armed with these reports, dispatched a formal protest to the Japanese through the international offices in Geneva promising continued protest and personal accountability for war crimes. The Japanese responded with denial but promises of issue investigation. Due to intensifying negative world opinion, continued American announcements concerning the camp conditions, and concern for post-war retribution, the Japanese vice-minister of war notified POW camp commanders of the following in March, 1944:

> In the light of recent intensified enemy propaganda warfare, if the present condition continues to exist, it will needlessly to add to the hostile feeling of the enemy and it will also be impossible for us to expect world opinion to be what we wish it to be. Such will cause an obstacle to our prosecution of moral warfare. Not only that, it is absolutely necessary to the health condition of POW's from the standpoint of using them satisfactorily to increase our fighting strength.[51]

Though it took a while to be felt in the camps, the information provided by Dyess, Mellnik, and McCoy with the assistance of the *Trout*, were ultimately successful.[52]

Once the war was over I eventually managed to get back to the States. Nobody at home knew what we had done on the submarine *Trout*, but my relatives had saved newspapers articles about the war that they thought might interest me. One of the papers, the *Chicago Tribune*, had a series of articles containing the edited reports about the prison camp conditions that Captain Dyess had provided. I became more fully aware of how atrocious and pervasive was the treatment experienced by the Allied prisoners at the hands of their Japanese captors. I certainly had a general idea from my many close conversations with these three men, but seeing it in black and white gave it a whole new reality for me.[53]

During the war Submarine Squadron Six was comprised of twelve subs six with names beginning with the letter "T," and six with the letter "G." The *Trout* was one of the boats in this squadron and one of the "Gs" was the USS *Grenadier* (SS 210). She was scuttled off Penang, on April 22, 1943, after being damaged by Japanese aircraft and the crew was taken prisoner by the Japanese; Edgar Lou Poss, Radioman First Class, my good friend, was one of them. Edgar

Chicago Tribune Article
Public Domain Image

survived the prison camp experience and returned to the States. In the post-war years, now Chief Poss and I were assigned to the USS *Spikefish* (SS 404). Working in close proximity to Ed Poss I had a "front row seat" opportunity to learn more about life in a Japanese POW camp. Ed would not always talk freely about the subject but if I started him talking about an unrelated subject often I could little by little lead the conversation toward his POW camp experiences. One of the things he confirmed was something we had been told in the Philippines by Commander Chick Parsons. Parsons said that Japanese prison camp officials had declared they would put to death ten prisoners for every one that escaped. This was to deter prison escapes by instilling fear of harsh retaliation. The calculation of this horrible equation went through my mind more than once on the *Trout* on the trip back from Davao Bay. Had I played a part in what might have been the ultimate execution of thirty Allied prisoners because I helped three escape?

Ed actually helped ease some of this guilt for me by relating his experiences. He said that when an escape took place, even in another camp, somehow the word was passed through the grapevine to the POW population. They always became very tense anticipating the reprisal to come. The guards definitely became more belligerent, verbally and physically abusive, and intimidating. "You no good American soldiers leave honorable Japanese camp and honorable Japanese care," he remembered one guard shouting at him. Their already meager food rations were further reduced and routine casual conversations, previously allowed, were curtailed; the word 'escape' would not dare be mentioned out loud. Chief Poss confirmed the increase in anger and abuse, the decrease in food and liberties, and the general atmosphere of imminent retaliation was present but also confirmed that he never knew of the 'ten-for-one' punishment being carried out.

Our three passengers made a great impact on the conditions in the Japanese POW camps. Though the conditions within the camps, by anyone's measure, were still horrible, the worst of the atrocities ended once Dyess' and the other's reports became public. Dyess did not live long enough to fully know the good he had done. He died in a plane crash on December 22, 1943, the same year as his liberation. After discharge from the hospital, Captain Dyess was emphatic about returning to active duty. He was assigned to the 337th Fighter Squadron to fly and test the P-38 Lightning. Brett A Manis II, 7th Bomber Wing historian at Dyess Air Force Base described the tragic accident that ended Dyess's life:

Dyess was killed during training when his P-38's engine caught fire. Dyess chose not to bail out so his aircraft would not crash into populated areas of Burbank, CA. Attempting to land on an open stretch of pavement, Dyess had to avoid an oncoming vehicle and crashed his P-38, dying on impact. He is buried in his hometown of Albany, TX.[54]

He didn't get to finish the book, but what had been completed was published with the title, *The Dyess Story* by G.P. Putnam's Sons, New York; I have a copy of it which I still treasure. A large airbase near Abilene, Texas was built at the beginning of the Cold War and it bears his name. Dyess Air Force Base opened as Abilene Air Force Base on April 15, 1956 and was renamed on December 1 of that same year. The base continues in operation to this day. Dyess received the Distinguished Flying Cross and the Distinguished Service Cross and was promoted to Lt. Colonel before his untimely death.[55]

Stephen M. Mellnik, who had been on General MacArthur's staff in the Philippines as an artillery expert prior to his capture, continued in the Army after his escape and rescue. He was awarded the Distinguished Service Cross and the Silver Star for his work developing the Philippine guerilla movement. After the war Mellnik held a number of positions in the War Department, the Army War College, the U. S. European Command, and the U. S. Army Air Defense School. He retired in 1963 as a General. He authored the book, Philippine War Diary: 1939-1945 which was published in 1969.[56]

Melvin H. McCoy also completed his military career, retiring as a Rear Admiral. Once the war was over and his cryptographic duties were over, McCoy served in various capacities including one as captain of the USS *Markab* (AD 21), a *Hamul*-class destroyer tender.

McCoy also received the Distinguish Service Cross. The citation for his award reads, in part:

> ...for extraordinary heroism in connection with military operations against an armed enemy as a Prisoner of War of the Japanese in the Philippine Islands during the period 4 April 1943 through 9 July 1944. Lieutenant Commander McCoy was one of ten men including two Naval Officers, three Air Corps Officers, and two Marine Corps Officers who escaped after nearly a year in captivity after the fall of Bataan and Corregidor. The ten men evaded their captors for days until connecting with Filipino Guerillas under Wendell Fertig. The officers remained with the guerillas for weeks, obtaining vital information which they carried with them when they were subsequently evacuated by American submarines. Their escape was the only mass escape from a Japanese prison camp during the war.[57]

Commander Charles "Chick" Parsons, U. S. Navy, our unexpected forth passenger, had been a businessman in the Philippines before the Japanese occupation. Briefly incarcerated, he was released after masqueraded as a Panamanian diplomat in Manila. He managed to get his family out of Manila and back to the States then immediately return to work for MacArthur as liaison to the guerila forces in the islands. He made eight forays into the Philippines transported there by submarine, several times on the *Trout*. He received for his service and dedication to the Philippines the Navy Cross (two awards), the Distinguished Service Cross, the Bronze Star Medal, the Philippine Medal of Valor, the Philippine Legion of Honor, and Order of St. Sylvester (one of five Orders of Knighthood awarded directly by the Pope). After the war he returned to the Philippines to resume his business pursuits which, ironically, including assisting the Japanese in rebuilding some of their damaged factories and businesses.[58]

Finally, a comrade of these three men, our expected forth passenger who elected to remain behind in the Philippines, was Samuel C. Grashio, a USAF pilot in the same squadron commanded by Dyess. After serving with the Mindanao guerrillas under the command of Lt. Col. Wendell Fertig, he was eventually extracted from the Philippines on another submarine, the USS *Bowfin* (SS 287), in September of 1943. Grashio served in the Army for twenty-five years retiring at the rank of colonel in 1965. He also received the Distinguished Service Cross and the Silver Star and co-authored,

Return to Freedom: The War Memoirs of Colonel Samuel C. Grashio U.S.A.F. with Bernard Nordling.[59]

The last character of this heroic story to discuss is the USS *Trout*. Her part in this tale has been described here but the *Trout* continued to fight on for a while after this mission was over. After a successful tenth patrol following the rescue mission the *Trout* was sent to the Mare Island Navy Shipyard for modernization and overhaul. She

Captain Samuel C. Grashio
holding Filipino dagger.
Public Domain Photo; The Dyess Story,
G.P. Putnam's Sons, 1944

returned to Submarine Division 162 at Pearl Harbor late in January 1944. I remained behind to attend an advanced radar school and the *Trout* departed on her eleventh war patrol on February 8. Japanese records indicate that one of their convoys was attacked by a submarine in what was the *Trout's* patrol area, on February 29. The convoy consisted of four large transports escorted by three *Yūgumo*-class destroyers. The 7,126 ton transport *Sakito Maru* was sunk and another large passenger-cargo ship was severely damaged. One of the destroyers detected the sub and dropped depth charges. When oil and debris came to the surface the destroyer dropped a final string of depth charges on the spot. The *Trout* was declared overdue and presumed lost on April 17, 1944.[60]

Years after the war was over, and once the Philippine government was back in control of their country, they presented the Philippine Republic Presidential Unit Citation to all of the boats and crews that had helped support the island's guerilla operations. The citation, issued on October 29, 1948, in part read as follows:

> The personnel of these units performed the dangerous mission of delivering critically needed supplies to guerilla forces in the Philippine Islands during the period of occupation by the enemy forces. These submarines and their brave personnel contributed to the alleviation of the sufferings of our oppressed people, strengthened the military effort of the guerillas and hastened the date of liberation from enemy domination.[61]

However, only I and a few of my shipmates received this citation directly. The *Trout* and eighty-one of the country's finest young men perished after giving their best for their country. I regret their passing and have thought of them every day for the last seventy years. I am proud to have been a member of the crew of the boat that was instrumental in relieving a bit of the suffering of so many men held prisoner far from hearth, far from home, but in the end, not so far from hope.

USS *Trout* (SS 202) at Hunters Point, 11 December 1943.
Submarine Force Museum & Library Archives

CHAPTER 5

───※───

SUBMARINE RADAR USED WWII IN THE PACIFIC AREA

BY J. "Deen" Brown, RMCM(SS), USN(Ret.)

MODEL SD - <u>Early 1942</u>

<u>Primary Purpose</u>: Air search, defense against aircraft.

<u>Secondary Purpose</u>: Large land mass detection.

<u>Operating Frequency</u>: VHF, Approximately 144 Mhz.

<u>Data Provided</u>: Range only, no azimuth data.

<u>Antenna</u>: Vertical polarized dipole, fed with two wire transition guide (no waveguide).

<u>Deficiencies</u>: Early antenna design left an area directly above the sub which was not illuminated thus aircraft directly overhead could

not be detected.

Later, redesign of the antenna corrected that problem; hemispherical illumination was provided.

Later in the war, Japanese developed effective countermeasures which they used in their patrol aircraft. They would home on our radar signal and attack.

Use of the SD Radar was rendered impractical. It was removed from most submarines prior to the war's end.

SD Radar Antenna[117]
http://pwencycl.kgbudge.com/S/d/
SD_air_warning_radar.htm
[accessed 2/25/2024].

MODEL SJ

SJ Radar on Submarine
http://www.ibiblio.org/hyperwar/USN/ref/Radar/Radar-1.html
[accessed 6/24/2023].

<u>Primary Purpose</u>: Surface search, ships and land

<u>Secondary Purpose</u>: Close range communication (Morse code) Detect other similar radars, homing operations.

<u>Operating Frequency</u>: 10 cm, (3000 Mhz) made possible by use of the British developed magnetron.

<u>Data Provided</u>: Azimuth bearing and range, used to provide data to solve the torpedo launch ballistic equation, e.g. input to the Torpedo Data Computer (TDC). Also use for ship navigation.

<u>Deficiencies</u>: Early models had only an "A" scope (indicator) thus a narrow sector of azimuth would be illuminated and searched. Antenna rotation provided full azimuth coverage sequentially (i.e. azimuth 360° coverage was not available in real-time.)

Eye strain was often a physical difficulty due to constant peering into the cathode ray tube "A" scope presentation. If the operator looked away while the antenna was rotating he could miss detection of an important target.

<u>Reliability</u>: Early models used vacuum tubes to directly pulse the magnetron. The demand on these tubes was severe thus tube failure rate was high. Thus modulator tubes (thyratron) were replaced after a few hours of operation. This was not only an inconvenience but often a failure occurred at a critical moment when radar data was of paramount importance.

Also, these vacuum tube designs generated a lot of heat. Often the ambient temperature in the sub was elevated in the area of the radar by these tubes. The result was increased operator discomfort and fatigue.

MODEL SJ Improvements:

Modulation network, thyratron tube pulsers were replaced with a ferromagnetic component called a "saturable reactor." Reliability of the system was improved by an order of magnitude.

Improved vacuum tubes (military specifications) further improved reliability.

Antennae radiation pattern was selectable; the main lobe could be divided in two closed spaced twin lobes (lobe switching) allowing the operator to determine the azimuthal bearing with precision.

Receiver sensitivity improved giving greater range.

Antenna rotation was converted to electric drive versus the old manual hand-cranked system.

The "A" scope presentation was augmented with the addition of a "Plan-Post-Indicator" (PPI). This was a significant improvement for submarine tactics. The boat now had a 360° polar presentation of the surrounding area (with antenna rotating) and could maintain a track plot of multiple targets.

Post War Assessment:

The MODEL SJ series radars served the submarine fleet admirably throughout World War II. However, late in the war, the last year or so, the Japanese obtained a rather feeble ability to detect the 10 cm radars. Accordingly, our subs used the radar judiciously and were somewhat hampered by Japanese countermeasures.

LATER RADAR DEVELOPMENTS

MODEL SS

The MODEL SS radar was developed to counter the threat posed by the enemy's ability to detect the presence of the 10 cm radars.

Other advantages were gained by the use of a much higher operating frequency, e.g. 3 cm. The Axis countries' technology development lagged far behind that of the European and American allies. Submarines equipped with the MODEL SS could use this new radar at will with little fear of being detected.

Primary Features: Improved freedom from detection.

"A" scope and PPI presentations with PPI presentation remote from the operator.

Improved azimuth bearing resolution (due to higher operating frequency and antenna design, a modified parabola).

Deficiencies: Submarines had to operate on or near the surface to expose the antenna above water. This placed an operational constraint on the sub with the attendant dangers of collision and/or being detected.

Accordingly, a new periscope was developed containing a 3cm radar antenna. A sub so equipped could then obtain azimuthal bearings from the periscope and much improved range data from the radar improving operational freedom.

MODEL ST

This was a new radar that used miniaturized components which reduced the size and weight of the system. Otherwise, it was similar in operation to the MODEL SS.

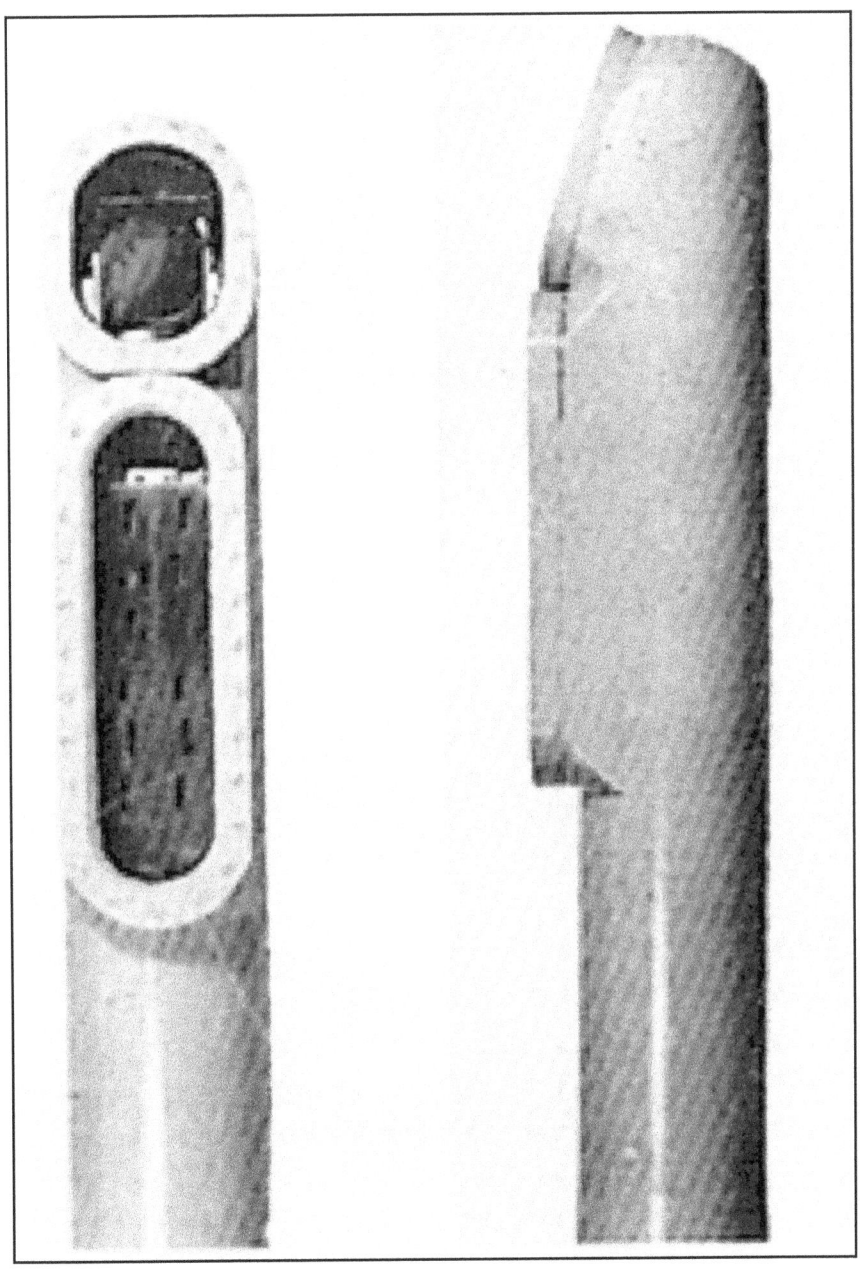

ST, STa, ST-1 SEARCH RADAR, range-determining
radar for submarine installation.
https://maritime.org/tech/radiocat/st.php [accessed 6/23/2023].

CHAPTER 6

---∿---

THE WAR PATROLS OF
THE USS *TROUT* (SS-202)

BY **Stephen Leal Jackson, PhD**

First War Patrol: November 28, to December 20, 1941
Lt. Cdr. F. W. Fenno, Commanding Officer

THE *TROUT* DEPARTED Pearl Harbor on November 29, 1941, and arrived to conduct a defensive patrol in an area around Midway Island on December 2 with the USS *Argonaut* (SS 166/SM-1). USS *Thresher* (SS 200), USS *Tambor* (SS 198) and USS *Triton* (SS 201) were also in the vicinity[62]. This began as a routine patrol although undoubtedly the increasing tensions between the United States and the Empire of Japan were understood by all. While on station, *Trout* received notice of the attack on Pearl Harbor and declaration of war thus this turned into *Trout's* first war patrol. The *Trout* reported that "On the night of December 7, 1941, the Island of Midway was shelled by two ships from the southwest for about 10 to 15 minutes. The *Trout* proceeded at full speed on the surface toward the western entrance to the channel but firing ceased before we arrived."[63] *Trout* inflicted no enemy damage on this initial, curtailed war patrol. Captain Fenno remarked in his war patrol report that "The men amused themselves by playing Acey-Ducey, cards, reading and sleeping. No organized recreation is needed. All hands gave a sigh of relief when we dove in the morning and relaxed."[64] However, things were different when the boat arrived at Pearl Harbor. As Theodore Roscoe wrote in United States Submarine Operations in World War II:

> One by one the other submarines arrived (at Pearl Harbor) – *Pollack*, *Pompano*, and *Plunger* from San Francisco, and later that month, *Tambor*, recalled from Wake, and *Trout* and *Argonaut* from Midway, and finally *Triton*. One by one they slid in from the sea, and their crews stared in shock at the harbor's devastation, and boats and crews were readied to go out again and fight the war.[65]

Second War Patrol: January 12 to March 3, 1942
Lt. Cdr. F. W. Fenno, Commanding Officer

Trout's second war patrol was one of the first submarine special missions and is the stuff of legend. The *Trout* left on a relief patrol to Corregidor to carry 3500 rounds of badly needed AA (anti-aircraft) ammunition. To make space inside the cramped vessel, the torpedo skids had to be removed and stored inside the superstructure. The ammo was then rapidly loaded, and the *Trout* put off to sea on the morning of January 20th.

After a brief stop at Midway to top-off the diesel fuel, *Trout* made her way and arrived at Corregidor on February 3rd. Manila Bay was an active war zone; rather than moving calmly to the pier *Trout* waited on the bottom until nightfall when a patrol boat could lead her in relative safety through the minefield. The sky was alive with Japanese warplanes and the tracers arcing up from American anti-aircraft batteries. The *Trout* crew, aided by a group of Philippine Scouts, leapt to the task of unloading the ammunition, one round at a time, hand to hand, through narrow hatches while war raged in the skies above.

The generous crew also unloaded food and supplies they could spare like fruit, canned food, and cigarettes. Offloading complete, the torpedo rooms had to be made operational once again. The six skids had to be manhandled back into position without the aid of cranes or other mechanical assistance. The crew loaded the six 900-pound skids, and two 3,000-pound torpedoes slow enough to complete the load safely, but with enough haste to get the *Trout* promptly ready to leave her vulnerable position, observable and near helpless tied to the pier.[66]

While on the way to the Philippines, Captain Fenno determined that the *Trout* could use more ballast. Once unloaded, he asked the Corregidor Naval Headquarters for twenty-five tons of ballast; sandbags were the captain's first choice as they could be moved around to adjust the boat's trim. Unfortunately, sandbags were the one thing the shore defenders could not sacrifice as all were in use improving shore defenses. However, could the captain use an equivalent weight of gold bars and silver coins? Weight is weight so the captain accepted. Trout took on board:

Two tons of gold bars. And 18 tons of silver pesos, plus stacks of negotiable securities and bags of vital State Department documents and U.S. Mail. Throughout the night of February 4th, in a dark scene lit by the gunfire on Bataan, gleaming yellow bars and clinking sacks of silver were stowed in the submarine's holds.[67]

It might have been perfectly reasonable after a successful special mission and after being loaded with the Philippine government's treasury and valuable State Department documents for the *Trout* to proceed cautiously back to Pearl Harbor. But the *Trout* was a warship in a warzone, so Captain Fenno proceeded to conduct a brief war patrol in the East China Sea. Five days out of Corregidor the Trout conducted a submerged attack on a Japanese freighter. Three torpedoes were fired, and two explosions sent the cargo ship to the bottom. After the war, this vessel was identified as the *Chuwa Maru*, 2,718 tons. The *Trout* also reported sinking a 200-ton Patrol Craft off the Bonin Islands, but this was not able to be verified.[68]

On February 10 *Trout* was ordered back to Pearl Harbor. On arrival her unusual cargo was offloaded and transferred to the USS *Detroit* (CL-8). The *Detroit* delivered the gold, silver, and securities to the United States Treasury Department in San Fransisco where it remained for the duration of the war. In an unusual conclusion to

Trout crew unload the load of gold and silver rescued from Corregidor
Submarine Force Museum & Library Archives

this unusual mission, all crew members were awarded the Army Silver Star suggested by General Douglas MacArthur as a reward for rendering assistance to his beloved Philippines.[69]

Third War Patrol: March 24 to May 17, 1942
Lt. Cdr. F. W. Fenno, Commanding Officer

In March the *Trout*, now unencumbered from the vast wealth of gold and silver, left on patrol with three other boats: *Thresher*, *Grayling*, and *Tambor*. Since U.S. codebreakers reported no Japanese capital ships around the Marshalls or Truk, only the *Tambor* was sent to that area; the remaining three boats heading for the seas around the Japanese home islands.[70] After several unsuccessful attacks, *Trout* and *Thresher* headed for what the war patrol reports cryptically called the "special patrol area." In fact, these two submarines were tasked to act as forward weather and enemy activity scouts for the upcoming Doolittle Raid on the Japanese home islands. These boats were to report on unfavorable weather conditions for a low-level, VFR (visual flight rules) attack by the sixteen B-25B medium bombers that would be launched from the carrier USS *Hornet* (CV 8).[71] These two boats were to report by exception; only if the weather was bad or if enemy fleets sortied. As it turned out, neither boat had to make a report as the weather remained fine and the enemy unaware and the raid achieved most if not all of its goal. Though the actual damage to Japanese infrastructure was slight, the morale boost for the American people was incalculable. The Navy commander of the raid, Admiral Halsey noted that the raid was "one of most courageous deeds in all military history."[72]

After being released from station, the *Trout* continued its war patrol, beginning by aggressively pursuing enemy commerce vessels east of Cape Shionomisaki and Cape Ichie (both off the most southerly point of the island of Honshu) and later around the Kii Channel.[73] The *Trout* engaged in twelve separate attacks, firing twenty-one torpedoes at eight different ships. The war patrol report identified five ships sunk for over 30,000 tons. Later reports only confirmed two ships sunk; the remaining targets may have been damaged or missed altogether. The two confirmed kills were:

May 2, 1942:	*Uzan Maru*	Cargo Ship	5,014 tons
May 4, 1942:	*Kongosan Maru*	Converted Gunboat	2,119 tons[74]

Though the official record trimmed *Trout's* tally of tonnage, this was still a very successful war patrol. In addition to the damage inflicted on enemy shipping, their support of the Doolittle Raid, though only in a "ready to serve" mode, showed them ready to provide vital information if the need had arisen that potentially saved one of America's precious aircraft carriers.

This was Mr. Deen Brown's first war patrol onboard *Trout*.

Forth War Patrol: May 21 to June 14, 1942
Lt. Cdr. F. W. Fenno, Commanding Officer

Trout's next war patrol was yet another mission destined to appear on newspaper headlines around the world. The Battle of Midway was arguably the turning point of the Pacific war and beginning of a more defensive battle strategy by the Imperial Japanese fleet. If the American submarines played purely a supporting role it was only because the American surface fleet performed unexpected well landing a devastating blow especially to the Japanese aircraft carriers. After the war, Japanese Captain Hisashi Ohara, former executive officer of the aircraft carrier *Soryu*, sunk at Midway, reflected on what the impact of the loss of four aircraft carriers had on the war plans of the Imperial Japanese Navy:

> Loss of the carriers meant loss of control of the air. We did not think we could capture Midway after we lost control of the air so we returned to Japan. The loss of the carriers and the planes also slowed up the occupation of the Solomons.[75]

The Japanese retreat rendered the American submarines mission unnecessary. The submarines were formed into Task Force 7 comprised of nineteen boats divided into three sub-groups. The *Trout* was part of Task Group 7.1 which contained twelve submarines. In addition to the *Trout* the group contained:

USS *Cachalot*
USS *Flying Fish*
USS *Tambor*
USS *Grayling*
USS *Nautilus*
USS *Grouper*
USS *Dolphin*
USS *Gato*
USS *Cuttlefish*
USS *Gudgeon*
USS *Grenadier*[76]

An indication of the condition of the American submarine service is evidenced by the age of the boats in this Task Group. There were a few *Gato* class boats, the most modern and a true fleet boat, many *Tambor* class boats like the *Trout* and *Tambor* itself, and some much older boats like the *Dolphin* and *Nautilus*. The *Nautilus* was from the *V-5* (*Narwal*) Class and had originally been named the USS *V-6* before renaming and modernization in 1931. Old or new, these doughty boats were ready to perform the task assigned.

The twelve boats in Task Group 7.1 arrayed themselves in a fan shape covering an arc from due north to south – southwest of Midway Island to prepare a defense against an anticipated invasion and landing. Task Group 7.2, comprised of three submarines patrolled an area between Midway and Oahu, prepared for a Japanese change of plans. Task Group 7.3, with four boats, patrolled north Oahu to protect the Hawaiian Islands. Though their contribution was diminished by the dominant strategy of the American fleet, a few boats did make an impact. The most noted was the death blow that the *Nautilus* delivered to stricken Japanese aircraft carrier *Soryu*. Additionally, on June 9th the *Trout* two survivors of the Japanese heavy cruiser *Mikuma*, found on a life raft from the sunken ship, that initially held seventeen. These may have been the first Japanese sailors to be taken prisoners during the war.[77]

The *Trout* returned to Pearl Harbor on June 14, 1942.

Fifth War Patrol: August 27 to October 13, 1942
Lt. Cdr. Lawson Paterson "Red" Ramage, Commanding Officer

Trout, now under the command of "Red" Ramage, left Pearl Harbor and headed for her assigned patrol area around Truk via the Marshall Islands to join the Truk blockade.[78] Arrived at and began reconnoitering the southern approaches to Truk on September 9th. Trout was apparently spotted the next day, either by a plane through the clear watch or when she did a periscope observation. Bombs were heard at a small distance perhaps from a observation plane and twenty minutes later several patrol boats commenced a depth charge attack. Over the next hour the patrol boats dropped forty-five depth charges; while none caused any damage, some, according to the war patrol report, were "a little too close for comfort." [79] Patrol boats continued to harass the *Trout* as the captain noted:

> At 0705 (September 10) heard first of four explosions which occurred at 10 minute intervals. Sighted our "constant companion", the smoking patrol boat. From then on one, two, or three patrol boats were constantly in sight and difficult to avoid.[80]

Late in the day on the 11th *Trout* sighted a large transport and commenced an attack. Periscope observation detected an escorting destroyer, and the periscope was lowered. Almost immediately two large explosions from aircraft bombs close astern rocked the boat. The after torpedo room was blacked out with the exception of emergency lighting and trim control became difficult. Attempting one more firing observation the *Trout* was shaken by six close-in depth charges and decided to "go deep and get clear". Thirty more depth charges were dropped until the boat finally got clear after sunset. The captain noted "a very disappointing day."[81]

On September 21st the *Trout* found a likely target, a naval auxiliary "with high gun platforms fore and aft." A spread of three torpedoes were fired from the after torpedo room. The first struck the ship and it appeared to break in two. The remaining two torpedoes hit the after section and the enemy ship went under. The victim was later identified as the converted net tender *Koei Maru*, 863 tons.[82]

On September 28th *Trout* was back on blockade patrol when she observed a carrier group consisting of two destroyers, two light cruisers, and the aircraft escort carrier *Taiyō*. After gaining a favorable fired position, the *Trout* fired five torpedoes at the carrier. The *Taiyō* was traveling faster than thought and only a single torpedo hit and damaged the carrier which was able to make Truk lagoon and effect repairs. The *Taiyō* would be attacked by three American submarines throughout the war and would finally be sunk by the USS *Rasher* (SS-269) on August 10th, 1944. A single torpedo struck the aft end of the carrier and ignited the aviation gasoline tank. The *Taiyō* sank in less than half an hour with a loss of life more than 800 men.[83]

On October 3rd, with their patrol drawing to a close, *Trout* was reconnoitering Otta Pass, the southern entrance to Truk Lagoon. After taking an observational fix, the periscope was lowered and immediately "a tremendous explosion close aboard which shook ship violently."[84] As the *Trout* sought deep water, a second explosion was felt but with no real effect. The first bomb had damaged

Trout received 11 battle stars for World War II service and Presidential Unit Citation for her second, third, and fifth war patrols.
Public domain image, Author's Collection

both periscopes to the point where they were rendered inoperable. This effectively ended their war patrol and the *Trout* headed for Brisbane, Australia for repairs. *Trout* moored alongside the submarine tender USS *Griffin* (AS 13) on October 13th.[85]

Sixth War Patrol: October 26 to November 23, 1942
Lt. Cdr. Lawson Paterson "Red" Ramage, Commanding Officer

Trout left Brisbane for a patrol area south of Gatukai Island in the New Georgia Group. After a quiet time on station *Trout* was ordered to the area north of Indispensable Strait, roughly north of Guadalcanal Island, to engage the *Kirishima*, a Kongo Class Japanese battleship. On November 13th *Trout* encountered *Kirishima* and achieved a favorable set-up. Five torpedoes were fired at the battleship but missed either passing astern or beneath the ship which at no time showed any indication of knowing they were under attack. An escorting destroyer made a desultory run at the *Trout*, dropping a mere two depth charges before moving off and rejoining the *Kirishima*.[86]

On November 19th *Trout* headed back to Brisbane, arriving on the 23rd. After minor repairs were accomplished by the submarine tender USS *Sperry* (AS 12) the boat headed to Fremantle for a change of station. At Fremantle, more extensive repairs and refitting were performed by the submarine tender USS *Pelias* (AS 14) to prepare *Trout's* next war patrol.

Seventh War Patrol: December 29, 1942, to February 25, 1943
Lt. Cdr. Lawson Paterson "Red" Ramage, Commanding Officer

Trout was directed to a patrol area off North Borneo via Makassar Strait. On January 11, 1943, a large Japanese tanker was sighted at moored off Miri, northwest Borneo. *Trout* had not had good luck finding enemy targets, so this sighting was very welcome. The tanker was inside the "ten-fathom curve" meaning that she was in water too shallow to permit a submerged attack. The tanker had been sighted in full daylight, so Ramage decided to wait in deep water until darkness and then attempt a surface attack. After 1930 *Trout* surfaced and began her approach. At about 1,700 yards from the tanker three torpedoes were fired two of which struck the tanker and exploded while the third malfunctioned at about 1,000 yards. *Trout* turned and fired one more torpedo from the after room which failed to explode.[87]

There was no doubt of the efficacy of the attack as massive primary and secondary explosions and the crew observed as "the tanker vomited spurts of dazzling flame." The war patrol report noted:

> Explosion on target accompanied by flames. Heavy explosion and brilliant flash on target – the shock was felt distinctly throughout this ship. Two more bright flashes on target followed by another at 2228.[88]

Though official post-war investigation failed to confirm the sinking of a large tanker at Miri, there is no doubt that the tanker was at least damaged enough to destroy its cargo and eliminate its war time usefulness for some time. Whether the damaged hulk was able to be salvaged is unknown, but this was undoubtedly a successful attack for the *Trout*.[89]

In the early hours of January 21st, she observed a "hump" on the horizon while patrolling off of the Indo-China coast. After closing with the target, it was determined to be a sub-chaser, apparently looking for *Trout* after receiving an air reconnaissance report, so she was given a wide berth. Shortly after sunrise a cargo ship was sighted, and *Trout* went to battle stations and began a zig-zagging approach. At 0738 two torpedoes were fired from the stern tubes and one hit the target just aft amidship which immediately began to settle by the stern and the screws stopped. Within minutes the cargo ship sank by the stern. The name of this *maru* was not determined but its sinking was confirmed as a cargo ship of 2,984 tons.[90]

One week later a perfect set-up and attack execution was thwarted by dud torpedoes. Trout attacked what was believed to be the Thai ship, *Phra Ruang*, the former HMS *Radiant*, a British destroyer built in 1916.[91] Ramage noted:

> Fired three torpedoes at 900 yards range 95-105 port track – observed torpedo tracks running true – could not have missed – no explosions – all DUDS!![92]

Luck improved, however, when, on February 7th, the tanker *Nisshin Maru No. 2* was discovered while patrolling off Miri, North Borneo. This was again a ship, mooring in shallow water so the attack plan was not immediately obvious. Ramage opted for a submerged attack firing two torpedoes and hearing one explosion as *Trout* moved out of the area. The tanker opened up with their deck gun, some round dropping quite close by, and a patrol boat engaged in a brief depth charge attack; neither caused any damage to the boat. The condition of the target could not be ascertained. However, any damage was easily repaired as the post-war records indicated that the *Nisshin Maru No. 2* continued in service for another year before she was scrapped.[93]

One week later, when sailing out of a rain squall, *Trout* comes across the Japanese ship *Hirotama Maru*. Ramage believed he had discovered a tanker, but the *Hirotama Maru* was an auxiliary transport that began its pre-war career as a cargo ship. Two torpedoes were fired at a range of 700 yards. The first torpedo "hit forward blowing bow off target *Hirotama Maru* – tanker – the second was a DUD!![94] When the ship, although damaged, could still maneuver Ramage called for battle surface and opened on the target with her deck guns. After some problems with the deck gun and several *Trout* crewmen wounded by return machine gun fire, *Trout* headed off while preparing torpedoes in the forward and after torpedo rooms. Still on the surface *Trout* fired one torpedo from the after room which found its mark. The *Hirotama Maru* sank bow first, stern up, screws still turning; she was listed at 1,911 tons. Seven crewmen were injured in this attack.[95]

No other actions occurred during the remainer of this patrol and the *Trout* arrived in Freemantle on February 25th, 1943.

Eighth War Patrol: March 22 to May 3, 1943
Lt. Cdr. Lawson Paterson "Red" Ramage, Commanding Officer

On this war patrol *Trout* was directed to proceed to *Soebi-ketjil* Island, just northwest of Borneo in the Riau Archipelago, conduct a six-day patrol while conducting a mine-laying operation in the Api Passage.[96] On April 4th she encountered a Japanese naval auxiliary, 3,500 tons and fired three torpedoes at 1000-yard range. One torpedo struck the target amidships, but only resulted in a "20 ft. plume of water just abaft amidships where the torpedo hit and air flask exploded. No warhead detonation."[97] A fourth torpedo was fired but the target apparently saw the wake and headed for shallow water. The attack was broken off as no viable shot was possible.

The next day the *Trout* again gained a target and after a long chase again fired three torpedoes at 1,400 yards that all missed. The enemy ship obviously saw the torpedoes or heard them explode in shallow water at the end of their run, as it began exercising its deck guns, but to no effect. *Trout* then headed to Api Passage to begin mining operation.

On April 7th the mining operation began at 1955. WWII submarines and their captains were not fond of minelaying operations for several reasons. First, since they were deployed from the torpedo tubes and mines were stored in the torpedo rooms, submarines involved in mining carried a much-reduced inventory of torpedoes. Second, since mines were generally deployed while the boat was on or close to the surface, these were inherently more dangerous for a fragile vessel that relies on stealth and the safety of the depths for successful operations. Last, while important to the war effort and, by reports, quite effective, the victims of these mines could not be credited to the submarine that laid the mines. Since the assessment of a successful patrol was mainly determined on tonnage sunk, this was a source of minor irritation for submarine captains. One exception to this was when Roy Benson, commanding USS *Trigger* (SS 237) had the pleasure of observing a Japanese patrol boat explode and sink after hitting one of his freshly laid mines.[98]

The operation was completed on April 8th at 0133 after 23 mines had been deployed and *Trout* dived and left the area to proceed to her patrol area west of *Soebi-ketjil* Island. There were only eight torpedoes remaining onboard; five were in the after torpedo room and three in the forward. Under cover of darkness *Trout* surfaced and transferred one torpedo to the forward room "to equalize distribution in order to have all torpedoes in the tubes."[99]

On April 18th *Trout* sighted a 3,000-ton *maru* at Dungun Anchorage with heavy stack smoke signaling preparation for getting underway. Once the maru got underway, *Trout* swung around to achieved firing position and fired a total of four torpedoes from the after room. Though the range was only 800 yards, no hits were achieved, and no end-of-run explosions were heard. Target zig-zagged away and *Trout* broke off the attack. At 1409 on the same day *Trout* attacked what she believed to be a tanker. Three torpedoes were fired but none found their mark. It was determined that "the size of the target had been grossly overestimated and that it was actually only a 2000-ton ship flying the Thaian Naval Ensign, later identified as the *Sumui*."[100] With only a single torpedo remaining, Ramage terminated the patrol and began the return to Freemantle.

On April 23rd after clearing the Sibutu Passage, the masts of two small ships were sighted. *Trout* dived and gained a position head of the two targets, identified as trawlers. Commenced Battle Surface and the trawlers responded by running up "all available Jap colors." *Trout* opened fire with her 3-inch deck gun and the 50- and 20-mm guns; the trawlers responded with machine gun fire. Both targets were soon "blazing from stem to stern." After one of the trawlers sank and the other a was burning wreck, *Trout* suspended the attack and resumed her transit to Fremantle where she arrived on May 3rd, 1943.[101]

ARLA 18. PHILIPPINE ISLANDS - SULU ARCHIPELAGO - TAWI TAWI ISLANDS - SIBUTU ISLANDS -
SIBUTU ISLAND - SIBUTU PASSAGE. (App. Lat. 4° 50' N. - Long. 119° 40' E.) Gun attack
& burning of two Jap trawlers by USS Trout, 4-23-43, south Sibutu Passage. Lens opening,
22; shutter speed, 1/100; light conditions, bright; range, inf.   CL #176-166

Gun attack and burning trawler, from USS *Trout* (SS 202), 4-23-1943.
Submarine Force Museum & Library Archives

Gun attack and second burning trawler, from USS *Trout* (SS 202),
4-23-1943.
Submarine Force Museum & Library Archives

Nineth War Patrol: May 27 to July 20, 1943

Lt. Cdr. Albert Hobbs Clark, Commanding Officer

The boat's Executive Officer, LCDR Albert Hobbs Clark assumed command for the 9th war patrol. Clark was part of the commissioning crew, thus a "plankowner," and would make all eleven war patrols on the *Trout*.[102]

This war patrol was primarily a special mission, with opportunities before and after to hunt for Japanese shipping. The war patrol report was, by necessity, near silent on the specifics of this mission. In the report's introduction it stated that after completing a six day patrol *Trout* should:

LCDR Albert Hobbs Clark
*Submarine Force Museum &
Library Archives*

THENCE PROCEED TO SOUTH COAST MINDANAO TO ARRIVE NOT EARLIER THAN 11 JUNE AND EXECUTE SPECIAL MISSION.[103]

The mission was an infiltration and extraction of personal and materials from the Japanese occupied Philippines. Details of this impactful mission are vividly described in the chapter; *Dark is the Harbor*.

The preliminary patrol period included one contact and attack on an auxiliary ship without damage or sinking of the vessel. On June 9th *Trout* fired three torpedoes from the stern room at the AK followed by a fourth. All were misses or duds as two "water piles" were reported, perhaps from exploding air tank but none of the torpedoes detonated. The target dropped two depth changes in a confused manners and fled under heavy smoke "apparently scared but undamaged" according to Clark.[104]

June 11th and 12th were spent on the first part special mission. Early on the 12th the boat dived and made a submerged patrol in the Moro Gulf to give the crew "much deserved rest after two busy nights." On June 15th, after an almost 8 hour chase to close and gain firing advantage, *Trout* fired three torpedoes at what would be later identified as the Japanese tanker ship *Sanruku Maru*, 3,000 tons. All three torpedoes struck the target, the fist and second eliminating the stern half of the ship and the third, "unexpectedly hit and left only the bow and foremast floating." No identification could be made at the time because the remains of the tanker "disappeared instantaneously with terrific explosion."[105]

On June 26th *Trout* came upon three, small coasters and gave chase. After achieving a position ahead of the three targets, battle surface was ordered, and the deck gun commenced the attack. The largest vessel broke up and sank leaving a patch of debris and oil. The second target, a large trawler, was dead in the water, abandoned, burning, and sinking. *Trout* focused on the third ship, a trawler type, and eventually sank that one as well. Detailed descriptions of these and other surface actions can be found in the chapter, Battle Surface.[106]

On July 2nd while on patrol near the Verde Island Passage, what was thought to be a "large tanker" was spotted and an attack commenced. After gaining position and swinging around for a bow shot, four torpedoes were fired from 2,700 yards. The first struck and may have "countermined" the second torpedo as a "heavy double explosion" was heard. The fourth torpedo struck the stern of the ship which began listing to starboard and sinking by the bow. The last observation showed the stern in the air with screws and rudder evident. After a heavy explosion no trace of the ship could be seen. The ship was later identified as Isuzu Maru, a cargo ship of 2,866 tons.[107]

On July 8th and 9th *Trout* began the second portion of the special mission. This involved extracting American officers who had formerly been prisoners of war of the Japanese. Their successful rescue and the testimony they provided to the President about the treatment of prisoners by the Japanese, eventually led to the mitigation of at least the most egregious practices.[108] The patrol and special mission having been successfully completed, *Trout* returned to Fremantle on July 20th.

General MacArthur Greets Escaped Heroes:
Left to right: Lt. Col. Dyess, Lt. Comdr. M. H. McCoy,
Gen. MacArthur, Major S. M. Melnik
Public Domain Photo; The Dyess Story, G.P. Putnam's Sons, 1944

Tenth War Patrol: August 12 to October 4, 1943

Lt. Cdr. Albert Hobbs Clark, Commanding Officer

The tenth war patrol took her through the Surigao and San Bernadino Straits on the way back to pearl Harbor. On August 25th a mast was sighted while sailing through the Molukka Passage. *Trout* diving and approached the contact which was a cargo-fisherman with "Japanese flag painted conspicuously on side." Battle surface was called for this relatively small target and the initial warning shot across the bow was ignored. Ten rounds from the deck gun into the ship's engine spaces brought the vessel to a stop. Members of the *Trout* crew boarded the disabled craft and searched for papers, maps, and other intelligence.[109]

The cargo, six tons of 1-inch wire, was definitely material of war Five Japanese crewmen were removed from the ship and demolition charges were set onboard. After the charges resulted in unsatisfying "smoke puffs," twelve rounds from the 3-inch gun finished the job and sent the ship to the bottom. About noon that day, three of the prisoners were installed in a dinghy taken from the Japanese ship and set loose off of Tidore Island; the remaining two prisoners were kept "for possible intelligence value." *Trout* then proceeded to a patrol area south of Sangihe Island.[110]

On September 9th, while conducting a surface and submerged patrol off of the eastern approach to Surigao Strait, an enemy submarine seemingly of the *I-62* (*Kaidai IV*) class was sighted. A short ten-minutes later *Trout* was able to fire three torpedoes which resulted in one large detonation and the stopping of the target's screws. Periscope observation showed the remainder of the waterspout and "much confusion on the bridge." *Trout's* sound man reported torpedo in the water and the boat made for 100 feet without incident. Upon return to periscope depth, no evidence of the Japanese submarine could be seen. *Trout* remained in the area until near sunset and then proceeded on patrol. The vessel sunk was thought to be the Japanese submarine *I-182*, 1,630 tons, but contradictory records indicate that the USS *Ellet* (DD-398) may have sunk the sub on about the same date.[111]

On September 22nd, one of the Japanese prisoners, S. Itshakawa, died of "self-imposed starvation." He became intractable after the torpedo attack on the 9th. He attacked one of his guards with "disastrous results to himself" due in part to the fact that, in the words of the captain, "he was the smallest Jap we ever saw." His hunger strike could not be ended even with the crew's attempted efforts with intravenous feeding and his body was sewn in a canvas sack and "thrown overboard."[112]

The next day around sunrise smoke was detected and the *Trout* moved to attack. Two stacks and the stack smoke from a third ship became visible. The leading ship was identified as a *Hokko Maru* class freighter "with a large deck load of small planes or trucks and the second as a *Atuta Maru* class transport. The view of the third ship was indistinct but was first thought to be a small freighter but eventually resolved itself to be an escort vessel making "some attempt at disguise." *Trout* fired three torpedoes at each of the freighters and was rewarded with two hits on each vessel. The escort responded and began a depth charge attack as the first ship's stern slipped under and lifeboats were launched. The second ship fired its deck guns "frantically;" less than 30 minutes after the attack began the first freighter sank and the transport was dead in the water, on fire, and abandoned by its remaining crew. *Trout* moved off, observing the transport nearly awash and using the ship to screen it from the escort. Two hours after the attack began a heavy explosion was heard and periscope observation showed no sign of the transport. The ships sunk were identified as cargo ship *Ryotuku Maru*, 3,483 tons and passenger-cargo ship *Yamashiro Maru*, 3,429 tons.[113]

At sunset *Trout* headed for Pearl Harbor and arrived there on October 4th, 1943.

Last War Patrol: February 8, to April 17, 1944 (presumed lost)
Lt. Cdr. Albert Hobbs Clark, Commanding Officer

Trout departed Pearl Harbor on February 8, 1944, on what would be her final patrol. After stopping at Midway to top-off her fuel tanks on February 16th, she headed out for her patrol area in the East China Sea. *Trout* was scheduled to be on patrol until March 27th and should have arrived at Midway around April 7th. Having received no contact from *Trout*, on April 17th the Commander Submarine Force – Pacific Fleet declared *Trout* "Overdue and Presumed Lost."[114]

What became of the *Trout*? On February 29th a Japanese convoy was attacked at position 22 degrees – 40' N, 131 degrees – 45' E by a submarine. The passenger-cargo ship *Aki Maru* was severely damaged and the passenger – cargo ship *Sakito Maru*, 7,126 tons, was sunk. *Sakito Maru* was serving as a troop transport the Japanese Army's 18th Infantry Regiment as part of a convoy transporting the 29th Division of the Kwantung Army to Guam. The ship sank with 2,358 soldiers and 52 crewmen of 3,500 men on board. Also lost were several light tanks and most of the regiment's equipment. The *Trout* was the only American submarine in the vicinity of the convoy on that date. The Japanese destroyer *Asashimo* dropped 19 depth charges on the assumed location of the attacking submarine and oil and debris floated to the surface. *Asashimo* dropped one more depth charge to conclude the attack. Since *Trout* did not report this engagement and was the only submarine in the area it is assumed that she was concluded the attack and was lost during or shortly after the depth charge attack.[115]

Trout Ship's Party, San Francisco Dec. 1943
Submarine Force Museum & Library Archives

Eighty-One men remain on Eternal Patrol on the USS *Trout* (SS-202)[118]

Name	Rate	Name	Rate
Abbot, R. E.	F2	Hoy, J. E.	MOMM1
Adams, A. W.	BKR3	Hughes, P. W.	S1
Barker, J. B. Jr.	GM3	Hughes, R. L.	CEMA
Beckley, C. V.	LTJG	Johnson, A. W.	TM2
Bennett, T. W. Jr.	RM3	Kaiser, R. W. Jr.	MOMM2
Boland, J. J.	CPHMA	Keltner, M. H.	ENS
Bond, R. V.	S1	Kerr, R. (n)	QM2
Brandt, N. A.	FC1	King, E. (n)	BM2
Brockman, R. J.	CTMA	Knutson, G. J.	MOMM1
Brownlow, E. (n)	CCSA	Kunstman, R. (n)	EM3
Callan, K. T.	EM3	Lewis, A. S.	STM2
Carrico, R. E.	LTJG	Magner, J. F.	MOMM1
Clark, A. H.	LCDR	Massett, P. J.	MOMM2
Clarke, J. B.	EM1	Mauer, L. L.	MOMM2
Coakley, J. B.	GM2	McDuffie, W. B.	SC3
Copt, L. J.	EM1	Million, F. A.	EM3
Corey, F. J.	EM2	Millner, C. C.	STM1
Crain, E. F. Jr.	ENS	Mollohan, G. D.	TM3
Crowley, J. R.	Y3	Murphy, T. J.	TM3
Cunningham, E. H. III	MMOM1	Myers, L. E. Jr.	LT
Decesare, F. P. Jr.	CRMA	Nearman, K. E.	RM2
Decker, F. J.	CMOMMA	Perry, R. R.	ENS
Dortch, W. H.	S2	Richardson, J. W.	CTMA
Ehlerding, J. G.	RM1	Rowan, L. R.	GM3
Ewell, J. E.	STM2	Ruder, J. E.	MOMM2
Eye, O. R.	TM3	Scott, K. I.	MOMM1
Festin, S. (n)	TM3	Sebring, S. R.	TM3
Finney, W. O.	MOMM2	Smith, A. L.	CMOMM
Frogner, G. I.	RM3	Stanford, W. W.	CMOMM
Frontino, J. N.	TM2	Swentzel, L. M.	F2
Frost, C. F.	MM1	Taylor, H. F.	EM3
Garrison, R. L.	TM2	Teisen, A. T.	MOMM1
Gaylord, W. H.	LT	Thoits, E. E.	TM3
Gionet, R. C.	MOMM2	Thurman, A. J.	S1
Gonyer, A. L.	SM1	Tierney, H. T	RT3
Gurney, H. R.	CYA	Tracy, J. T.	EM3
Gwynn, R. P.	S1	Walker, E. J.	SM3
Hall, O. (n)	EM1	Wilkowski, J. B.	SM2
Halterman, A. M.	TM1	Winter, W. A.	GM1
Hanford, S. J.	MOMM3	Woodworth, H. E.	LT
Harrison, D. W.	CEMA		

Eternal Father, strong to save, Whose arm hath bound the restless wave, Who bidd'st the mighty ocean deep Its own appointed limits keep, O hear us when we cry to thee For those in peril on the sea![116]

USS *Trout* (SS 202) heading out to sea.
Submarine Force Museum & Library Archives

EPILOGUE

JEWELDEEN (DEEN) BROWN, 96, of Fire Street, Oakdale, passed away at Beechwood Transitional Care in New London on April 14, 2019, after a brief illness. Born in Schell City, MO, he was a son of the late Edward and Perl (Anderson) Brown.

Mr. Brown was a man of quiet dignity, robust constitution, and fierce patriotism. He offered friends and acquaintances his quiet respect and it was returned in kind. He lived a full measure of life, and then some. A unique man from a sturdier era; we will not see his like again. Loving

Jeweldeen Brown, RMCM (SS), USN, (Ret.), c. 1995. *Author's Collection.*

husband, father, grandfather and great-grandfather, and faithful friend, mentor, and shipmate to many, he will be sorely missed.

SELECTED BIBLIOGRAPHY

Primary Sources

Books

Dyess, William E. *The Dyess Story*. New York: G. P. Putnam's Sons, 1944.

Grashio, Samuel C. and Bernard Norling. R*eturn to Freedom: The War Memoirs of Colonel Samuel C. Grashio U.S.A.F.* Spokane, WA: University Press, 1982.

Military Publications

United States Navy. *The Fleet Type Submarine – NAVPERS 16160*. Washington: US Government Printing Office, 1946, reprint by www.periscopefilm.com.

United States Submarine Losses – World War II. Washington: U. S. Government Printing Office, 1946. Revised and reissued as NAVPERS 15,784 in 1949.

Interviews by the Editor

Brown, Jeweldeen "Deen", Master Chief Radioman USN (ret.).
Interview by author, 17 January 2007, Montville, Connecticut.
Digital recording – transcribed.

Radioman on USS *Trout* for eight war patrols.

Magazines, Articles, Journals, and other sources

Zahl, Lt. Col. Harold A. and Major John W. Marchetti; "Radar on
50 centimeters", *Electronics*, Jan. 1946.

War Patrol Reports

United States Navy. Report of War Patrols. U. S. Navy Submarine
Force Museum, Groton, Connecticut and at https://maritime.
org/doc/subreports.php.

War Patrol Reports are available for every World War II submarine. These books contain the archived official post-patrol
report for each submarine.

Clark, A. H., commanding, "USS *Trout* (SS 202), Report of War
Patrol Number Nine". Commander Submarine Force Pacific
Fleet, 22 July 1943, typewritten and library bound; Book 202,
U. S. Navy Submarine Force Museum, Groton, Connecticut;
https://maritime.org/doc/subreports.php [accessed
2/25/2024].

Clark, A. H., commanding, "USS *Trout* (SS 202), Report of War Patrol Number Ten". Commander Submarine Force Pacific Fleet, 4 October 1943, typewritten and library bound; Book 202, U. S. Navy Submarine Force Museum, Groton, Connecticut; https://maritime.org/doc/subreports.php [accessed 2/25/2024].

Fenno, F. W., Jr., commanding, "USS *Trout* (SS 202), Report of War Patrol Number One". Commander Submarine Force Pacific Fleet, 27 December 1941, typewritten and library bound; Book 202, U. S. Navy Submarine Force Museum, Groton, Connecticut; https://maritime.org/doc/subreports.php [accessed 2/25/2024].

Fenno, F. W., Jr., commanding, "USS *Trout* (SS 202), Report of War Patrol Number Two". Commander Submarine Force Pacific Fleet, 6 March 1942, typewritten and library bound; Book 202, U. S. Navy Submarine Force Museum, Groton, Connecticut; https://maritime.org/doc/subreports.php [accessed 2/25/2024].

Fenno, F. W., Jr., commanding, "USS *Trout* (SS 202), Report of War Patrol Number Three". Commander Submarine Force Pacific Fleet, 17 May 1942, typewritten and library bound; Book 202, U. S. Navy Submarine Force Museum, Groton, Connecticut; https://maritime.org/doc/subreports.php [accessed 2/25/2024].

Fenno, F. W., Jr., commanding, "USS *Trout* (SS 202), Report of War Patrol Number Four". Commander Submarine Force Pacific Fleet, 14 June 1942, typewritten and library bound; Book 202, U. S. Navy Submarine Force Museum, Groton, Connecticut; https://maritime.org/doc/subreports.php [accessed 2/25/2024].

Hutchinson, E. S., commanding, "USS *Rasher* (SS 269), Report of War Patrol Number One". Commander Submarine Force Pacific Fleet, 24 November 1943, typewritten and library bound; Book 269, U. S. Navy Submarine Force Museum, Groton, Connecticut; https://maritime.org/doc/subreports.php [accessed 2/25/2024].

Munson, H. G. commanding, "USS *Rasher* (SS 269), Report of War Patrol Number Five". Commander Submarine Force Pacific Fleet, 3 September 1944, typewritten and library bound; Book 269, U. S. Navy Submarine Force Museum, Groton, Connecticut; https://maritime.org/doc/subreports.php [accessed 2/25/2024].

Ramage, L. P., commanding, "USS *Trout* (SS 202), Report of Fifth War Patrol". Commander Submarine Force Pacific Fleet, 13 October 1942, typewritten and library bound; Book 202, U. S. Navy Submarine Force Museum, Groton, Connecticut; https://maritime.org/doc/subreports.php [accessed 2/25/2024].

Ramage, L. P., commanding, "USS *Trout* (SS 202), Report of Sixth War Patrol". Commander Submarine Force Pacific Fleet, 23 November 1942, typewritten and library bound; Book 202, U. S. Navy Submarine Force Museum, Groton, Connecticut; https://maritime.org/doc/subreports.php [accessed 2/25/2024].

Ramage, L. P., commanding, "USS *Trout* (SS 202), Report of Seventh War Patrol". Commander Submarine Force Pacific Fleet, 25 February 1943, typewritten and library bound; Book 202, U. S. Navy Submarine Force Museum, Groton, Connecticut; https://maritime.org/doc/subreports.php [accessed 2/25/2024].

Ramage, L. P., commanding, "USS *Trout* (SS 202), Report of Eighth War Patrol". Commander Submarine Force Pacific Fleet, 8 May 1943, typewritten and library bound; Book 202, U. S. Navy Submarine Force Museum, Groton, Connecticut; https://maritime.org/doc/subreports.php [accessed 2/25/2024].

SECONDARY SOURCES

Books

Blair, Clay Jr. *Silent Victory: The U. S. Submarine War Against Japan*. New York: J. B. Lippincott, 1975.

Chun, Clayton K. S. *The Doolittle Raid 1942: America's First Strike Back at Japan*. Oxford, UK: Osprey Publishing, 2006.

de Bary, William Theodore. *Sources of East Indian Tradition: The Modern Period.* New York: Columbia University Press, 2008.

Hoyt, Edwin P. *Submarines at War: The History of the American Silent Service.* Brancliff Manor, NY: Stein and Day, 1983.

_____ *To the Marianas: War in the Central Pacific: 1944.* New York: Van Nostrand Reinhold Company, 1980.

Kerr, E. Bartlett. *Surrender and Survival: The Experience of American POWs in the Pacific 1941-1945.* New York: William Morrow and Company, Inc., 1985.

Knox, Donald. *Death March: The Survivors of Bataan.* New York: Harcourt, Brace, Jovanovich, 1981.

Mellnik, Stephen M. *Philippine War Diary: 1939-1945.* New York: Van Nostrand Reinhold Co., 1969.

Parker, Frederick D. *A Priceless Advantage: U.S. Navy Communications Intelligence and the Battles of Coral Sea, Midway, and the Aleutians.* Fort Meade MD: Center for Cryptologic History, National Security Agency, 1993.

Parshall, Jonathan and Anthony Tully. *Shattered Sword: The Untold Story of the Battle of Midway.* Lincoln, NE: Potomac Books, 2007.

Paige, R. M. *Monostatic Radar.* IEEE Trans. ASE no. ASE-13, No. 2, Sept. 1977.

Roscoe, Theodore. *United States Submarine Operations in World War II*. Annapolis, Maryland: United States Naval Institute, 1949.

Magazines, Articles, Journals, and other sources

Page, R. M., "Monostatic Radar" IEEE Trans. ASE, no. ASE-13, no. 2, Sept 1977.

Swan, William L., "The Japanese Occupation in Southeast Asia" *Journal of Southeast Asian Studies*, Vol. 27, No. 1, (Mar., 1996, 139-149).

Weir, Gary E., "The Search for an American Submarine Strategy and Design, 1919 – 1936", *Naval War College Review* Volume XLIV, Number 1, Sequence 333 (Winter 1991), 34 – 46.

Submarine Related Websites

https://www.baesystems.com/en-us/definition/what-are-iff-technologies

BAE Systems, Inc. is the U.S. subsidiary of BAE Systems plc.

http://www.combinedfleet.com/

The Internet site of the Imperial Japanese Navy Page.

http://www.cpf.navy.mil/news_images/special_projects/Wahoo/wahoo.htm

The Internet site of the U.S. Pacific Fleet Public Affairs Office, 250 Makalapa Drive, Building 81, Pearl Harbor, Hawaii, 96860-3131.

http://www.csp.navy.mil/ww2boats.htm

The Internet site of COMSUBPAC Public Affairs, 1430 Morton Street, Pearl Harbor, HI 96860-4664.

https://www.dyess.af.mil/Fact-Sheets/Display/Article/812832/dyess-history/

The Internet site of Dyess Air Force Base.

https://www.globalsecurity.org/military/world/thailand/navy-history-20c.htm

GlobalSecurity.org is the source of background information and developing news stories in the fields of defense, space, intelligence, WMD, and homeland security.

https://www.history.navy.mil/

The Internet site of the Naval History and Heritage Command.

http://www.ibiblio.org/hyperwar/PTO/Magic/COMINT-CoralSea/PartOne.html

The Public's Library and Digital Archive; Part One: The Battle of the Coral Sea

https://www.liverpoolmuseums.org.uk/maritime-museum

The Internet site of the National Museums – Liverpool.

http://www.oneternalpatrol.com/uss-trout-202.htm

On Eternal Patrol: Dedicated to all men lost while serving in the U.S. Submarine Force.

https://www.marineregions.org/gazetteer.php?p=details&id=16480

Marine Regions: an integration of the VLIMAR Gazetteer and the VLIZ Maritime Boundaries Geodatabase.

https://www.maritime.org/

The Internet Site of the San Francisco Maritime National Park Association.

https://www.nationalmuseum.af.mil/Visit/Museum-Exhibits/Fact-Sheets/Display/Article/196340/norden-m-9-bombsight/

The Internet site of the National Museum of the U.S. Air Force.

https://navalunderseamuseum.org/

The Internet site of the U.S. Naval Undersea Museum.

http://navsource.org/

The Internet site of the NavSource Naval History: Photographic History of the U.S. Navy.

http://www.navweaps.com/Weapons/WAMUS_Mine_Success.pdf

Naval Weapons, Naval Technology and Naval Reunions.

http://www.navy.mil/navydata/cno/n87/usw/issue_13/now_then.html

The Internet site of the Naval Historical Center, an official U.S. Navy web site.

http://pwencycl.kgbudge.com/S/d/SD_air_warning_radar.htm

The Pacific War Online Encyclopedia

https://www.smithsonianmag.com/history/without-chick-parsons-General-MacArthur-Never-Made-Return-Philip-pines-180964406/

The Internet site of the Smithsonian Magazine.

https://www.usna.edu/Chapel/navyhymn.php

U. S. Naval Academy Chapel

https://usnamemorialhall.org/index.php/
ALBERT_H._CLARK,_LCDR,_USN

U.S. Naval Academy Virtual Memorial Hall.

https://www.usni.org/magazines/proceedings/1960/january/
gold-ballast-war-patrol-uss-trout

The Internet site of the U. S. Naval Institute.

http://www.ussnautilus.org/

The Internet site of the Historic Ship Nautilus and U. S. Navy
Submarine Force Museum, Groton, Connecticut.

INDEX

ENDNOTES

1   The *Pelias* was a Type C3-class cargo ship designed by the United
    States Maritime Commission (MARCOM) in the late 1930s. The C-3s
    weren't designed for any specific service or trade but was more of a
    general-purpose ship that could be modified for any number of uses.
    http://www.navsource.org/archives/09/36/3614.htm [accessed
    7/6/2023].
2   300 feet, 92 meters.
3   F. W. Fenno, Jr., commanding, "USS *Trout* (SS 202), Report of War
    Patrol Number Two" (Commander Submarine Force Pacific Fleet,
    6 March 1942, typewritten and library bound; Book 202, U. S. Navy
    Submarine Force Museum, Groton, Connecticut); https://maritime.
    org/doc/subreports.php.
4   The Kii Channel. An entrance to Osaka Bay where the port facilities
    for Kobe and Osaka resided. https://www.marineregions.org/gazet-
    teer.php?p=details&id=16480 [accessed 6/24/2023].
5   https://www.nationalmuseum.af.mil/Visit/Museum-Exhibits/Fact-
    Sheets/Display/Article/196340/norden-m-9-bombsight/ [accessed
    6/23/2023].
6   F. W. Fenno Jr., "USS *Trout* (SS 202), Report of War Patrol Number
    Three".
7   F. W. Fenno Jr., commanding, "USS *Trout* (SS 202), Report of War
    Patrol Number Four" (Commander Submarine Force Pacific Fleet,
    14 June 1942, typewritten and library bound; Book 202, U. S. Navy
    Submarine Force Museum, Groton, Connecticut); https://maritime.
    org/doc/subreports.php.
8   L. P. Ramage, commanding. "USS *Trout* (SS 202), Report of War
    Patrol Number Five" (Commander Submarine Force Pacific Fleet, 13
    October 1942, typewritten and library bound; Book 202, U. S. Navy

Submarine Force Museum, Groton, Connecticut); https://maritime. org/doc/subreports.php.

9   Patrol Craft http://www.navsource.org/archives/12/01idx.htm [accessed 6/24/2023].

10   A. H. Clark, commanding, "USS *Trout* (SS 202), Report of War Patrol Number Nine" (Commander Submarine Force Pacific Fleet, 22 July 1943, typewritten and library bound; Book 202, U. S. Navy Submarine Force Museum, Groton, Connecticut);

11   Station CAST was the United States Navy signals monitoring and cryptographic intelligence fleet radio unit at Cavite Navy Yard in the Philippines, until Cavite was captured by the Japanese forces in 1942, during World War II from http://www.ibiblio.org/hyperwar/ PTO/Magic/COMINT-CoralSea/PartOne.html, [accessed 7/6/2023]; Frederick D. Parker, *A Priceless Advantage: U.S. Navy Communications Intelligence and the Battles of Coral Sea, Midway, and the Aleutians* (Fort Meade MD: Center for Cryptologic History, National Security Agency, 1993).

12   L. P. Ramage, commanding, "USS *Trout* (SS 202), Report of Seventh War Patrol" (Commander Submarine Force Pacific Fleet, 25 February 1943, typewritten and library bound; Book 202, U. S. Navy Submarine Force Museum, Groton, Connecticut); https://maritime. org/doc/subreports.php.

13   Ibid.

14   Identification Friend or Foe (IFF) Interrogators are electronic devices that emit an "interrogating" radio signal at one frequency, prompting an IFF Transponder to emit a reply signal at a different frequency, indicating that an approaching aircraft is "friendly." https://www.baesystems.com/en-us/definition/what-are-iff-technologies [accessed 6/24/2023].

15   *Gar's* eleventh war patrol; The Battle of Peleliu, codenamed Operation Stalemate, was fought between the United States and Japan in the Pacific Theater of World War II, taking place between September and November 1944. https://www.history.navy.mil/browse-by-topic/wars-conflicts-and-operations/world-war-ii/1944/peleliu.html [accessed 6/24/2023].

16   https://ussnautilus.org/the-lucky-cribbage-board/ [accessed 7/6/2023].

17   William Theodore de Bary, *Sources of East Asian Tradition: The Modern Period*, (New York: Columbia University Press, 2008), 622.

18   War patrol reports show *Trout* arriving in Brisbane on 13 October 1942 while *Sailfish* did not arrive until 1 November. This does not rule out the possibility of *Sailfish* escorting *Trout* to the Brisbane approaches and then proceeding on for another two weeks but there is no evidence of this currently available; L. P. Ramage, commanding,

"USS *Trout* (SS 202), Report of War Patrol Number Five" (Commander Submarine Force Pacific Fleet, 13 October 1942, typewritten and library bound; Book 202, U. S. Navy Submarine Force Museum, Groton, Connecticut), 8; https://maritime.org/doc/subreports.php.

19 L. P. Ramage, commanding, "USS *Trout* (SS 202), Report of War Patrol Number Six" (Commander Submarine Force Pacific Fleet, 23 November 1942 typewritten and library bound; Book 202, U. S. Navy Submarine Force Museum, Groton, Connecticut), 1; https://maritime.org/doc/subreports.php.

20 Ibid., 5.

21 Ramage, "USS *Trout* (SS 202), Report of War Patrol Number Six", 6.

22 http://www.maritime.org/doc/radar/part2.htm, Radar Operator's Handbook, U. S. GOVERNMENT PRINTING OFFICE: 1945-6388S9 [accessed 6/24/2023].

23 Ramage, "USS *Trout* (SS 202), Report of War Patrol Number Six, 6; https://maritime.org/doc/subreports.php.

24 H. G. Munson, commanding, "USS *Rasher* (SS 269), Report of War Patrol Number Five" (Commander Submarine Force Pacific Fleet, 3 September 1944), 10; https://maritime.org/doc/subreports.php.

25 Ibid.,10, 10a, 11.

26 http://www.combinedfleet.com/taiyo.htm [accessed 6/24/2023].

27 Munson, "USS *Rasher* (SS 269), Report of War Patrol Number Five", 23-35; COMSUBSPAC Patrol report No. 517, USS *Rasher* (SS-269), 1-2; https://maritime.org/doc/subreports.php.

28 William L. Swan. "The Japanese Occupation in Southeast Asia" *Journal of Southeast Asian Studies*, Vol. 27, No. 1, (Mar., 1996, 139-149), 139.

29 Donald Knox. *Death March: The Survivors of Bataan* (New York: Harcourt, Brace, Jovanovich, 1981), 175 – 184.

30 E. Bartlett Kerr. *Surrender and Survival: The Experience of American POWs in the Pacific 1941-1945* (New York: William Morrow and Company, Inc., 1985), 19 & 134.

31 Stephen M. Mellnik. *Philippine War Diary: 1939-1945* (New York: Van Nostrand Reinhold Co., 1969), 266 – 268.

32 Ibid., 266.

33 William E. Dyess, *The Dyess Story* (New York: G. P. Putnam's Sons, 1944), 16 – 17.

34 Fenno, "USS *Trout* (SS 202), Report of War Patrol Number Two", 2.

35 Clark, commanding, "USS *Trout* (SS 202), Report of War Patrol Number Nine", 1.

36 Ibid., 5.

37 Ibid., 15.

38 Samuel C. Grashio and Bernard Norling. *Return to Freedom: The War Memoirs of Colonel Samuel C. Grashio U.S.A.F.* (Spokane, WA:

University Press, 1982), 154 – 158.

39   Ibid., 151 & 153; https://www.smithsonianmag.com/history/with-out-chick-parsons-General-MacArthur-Never-Made-Return-Philip-pines-180964406/ [accessed 6/23/2023].

40   Dyess, *The Dyess Story*, 179.

41   Ibid., 167.

42   Clark, "USS *Trout* (SS 202), Report of War Patrol Number Nine", 5.

43   Ibid., 7 & 8.

44   Ibid., 9.

45   Lt. Col. Harold A. Zahl and Major John W. Marchetti; "Radar on 50 centimeters", *Electronics*, Jan. 1946, 98.

46   Mellnik. *Philippine War Diary: 1939-1945*, 191.

47   Clark, "USS *Trout* (SS 202), Report of War Patrol Number Nine", 13.

48   Ibid., 17.

49   Ibid., 1.

50   Kerr, *Surrender and Survival: The Experience of American POWs in the Pacific 1941-1945*, 162-163.

51   Ibid., 164.

52   Ibid., 162-164.

53   Grashio and Nordling. *Return to Freedom: The War Memoirs of Colonel Samuel C. Grashio U.S.A.F.*, 182 – 183.

54   Email from Brett A Manis II, 7th Bomb Wing historian at Dyess AFB, TX.

55   Ibid.; https://www.dyess.af.mil/Fact-Sheets/Display/Arti-cle/812832/dyess-history/ [accessed 6/23/2023].

56   Mellnik. *Philippine War Diary: 1939-1945*, back cover.

57   Headquarters: U.S. Army Forces in the Far East, General Orders No. 47 (1943).

58   https://www.smithsonianmag.com/history/without-chick-parsons-General-MacArthur-Never-Made-Return-Philippines-180964406/ [accessed 6/23/2023].

59   Grashio and Nordling. *Return to Freedom: The War Memoirs of Colonel Samuel C. Grashio U.S.A.F.*, 168 – 169.

60   Edwin P. Hoyt. *To the Marianas: War in the Central Pacific: 1944* (New York: Van Nostrand Reinhold Company, 1980), 240.

61   Philippine Republic Presidential Unit Citation issued to Jeweldeen Brown, 29 October 1948, AGB6 300.4 GO No. 500, author's collec-tion.

62   Theodore Roscoe, *United States Submarine Operations in World War II* (Annapolis, Maryland: United States Naval Institute, 1949), 8.

63   Fenno, "USS *Trout* (SS 202), Report of War Patrol Number One, Commander Submarine Force Pacific Fleet, 27 December 1941, type-written and library bound; Book 202, U. S. Navy Submarine Force

Museum, Groton, Connecticut, 2; https://maritime.org/doc/subreports.php.

64 Ibid., 3.
65 Roscoe, *Submarine Operations in World War II*, 21.
66 Fenno, "USS *Trout* (SS 202), Report of War Patrol Number Two", 2; Roscoe, *Submarine Operations in World War II*, 79; https://maritime.org/doc/subreports.php.
67 Roscoe, *Submarine Operations in World War II*, 80.
68 Ibid., 562.
69 https://www.usni.org/magazines/proceedings/1960/january/gold-ballast-war-patrol-uss-trout [accessed 2/1/2024].
70 Clay Blair, Jr. *Silent Victory: The U. S. Submarine War Against Japan* (New York: J. B. Lippincott, 1975), 190.
71 Clayton K. S. Chun. *The Doolittle Raid 1942: America's First Strike Back at Japan* (Oxford, UK: Osprey Publishing, 2006, 121.
72 Blair, Jr. Clay Blair, Jr. *Silent Victory: The U. S. Submarine War Against Japan*, 191.
73 Ibid., 190; Fenno, "USS *Trout* (SS 202), Report of War Patrol Number Three", 4.
74 Roscoe, *Submarine Operations in World War II*, 562.
75 Ibid., 133.
76 Ibid., 124, 125.
77 Ibid., 132; Jonathan Parshall and Anthony Tully, *Shattered Sword: The Untold Story of the Battle of Midway* (Lincoln, NE: Potomac Books, 2007), 142; *Trout* War Patrol Report, 4th War Patrol, page 3.
78 Roscoe, *Submarine Operations in World War II*, 158.
79 Ramage, "USS *Trout* (SS 202), Report of War Patrol Number Five", 1&2.
80 Ibid., 3.
81 Ibid.
82 Ibid., 5; Roscoe, *Submarine Operations in World War II*, 562.
83 *Trout* War Patrol Report, 5th War Patrol, 6; "IJN Chuyo: Tabular Record of Movement". *Imperial Japanese Navy Page. Combined Fleet. com* [accessed 3/8/2024].
84 Ramage, "USS *Trout* (SS 202), Report of War Patrol Number Five", 7.
85 Ibid., 8.
86 Ramage, "USS *Trout* (SS 202), Report of War Patrol Number Six", 6, 10, & 11.
87 Roscoe, *Submarine Operations in World War II*, 202.
88 Ramage, "USS *Trout* (SS 202), Report of War Patrol Number Seven", 5.
89 Roscoe, *Submarine Operations in World War II*, 202.
90 Ramage, "USS *Trout* (SS 202), Report of War Patrol Number

Seven", 7 & 8; Roscoe, *Submarine Operations in World War II*, 562.

91 https://www.globalsecurity.org/military/world/thailand/navy-history-20c.htm [accessed 2/10/2024].

92 Ramage, "USS *Trout* (SS 202), Report of War Patrol Number Seven", 10.

93 Ibid., 7 & 8, 14; http://www.combinedfleet.com/Nisshin_t.htm [accessed 2/10/2024]; *Hackett, Bob; Peter Cundall (2009).* "Japanese Oilers: IJN Nisshin Maru".

94 Ramage, "USS *Trout* (SS 202), Report of War Patrol Number Seven", 14.

95 Ibid., 14; http://www.combinedfleet.com/Hirotama_t.htm [accessed 2/10/2024]; Roscoe, *Submarine Operations in World War II*, 562.

96 L. P. Ramage, commanding, "USS *Trout* (SS 202), Report of Eighth War Patrol". Commander Submarine Force Pacific Fleet, 8 May 1943, typewritten and library bound; Book 202, U. S. Navy Submarine Force Museum, Groton, Connecticut, 1; https://maritime.org/doc/subreports.php.; http://www.navweaps.com/Weapons/WAMUS_Mine_Success.pdf, *The Submarine Review*, October 2007, *U. S. Submarine Mining Successes During WWII*, CDR John D. Allen, USN (Ret), p. 65-77 [accessed 2/11/2024].

97 Ramage, "USS *Trout* (SS 202), Report of War Patrol Number Eight", 6.

98 http://www.navweaps.com/Weapons/WAMUS_Mine_Success.pdf, *The Submarine Review*, October 2007, *U. S. Submarine Mining Successes During WWII*, CDR John D. Allen, USN (Ret), p. 69-70, [accessed 2/11/2024].

99 Ramage, "USS *Trout* (SS 202), Report of War Patrol Number Eight", 9.

100 Ibid., 14; http://www.navweaps.com/index_oob/OOB_WWII_Pacific/OOB_WWII_Ko-Chang.php [accessed 2/27/2024].

101 Ramage, "USS *Trout* (SS 202), Report of War Patrol Number Eight", 15-16, 18.

102 https://usnamemorialhall.org/index.php/ALBERT_H._CLARK,_LCDR,_USN [accessed 2/13/2024].

103 Clark, "USS *Trout* (SS 202), Report of War Patrol Number Nine", 1.

104 *Ibid.,* 5.

105 Clark, "USS *Trout* (SS 202), Report of War Patrol Number Nine", 7 & 8; Roscoe, *Submarine Operations in World War II*, 562.

106 Clark, "USS *Trout* (SS 202), Report of War Patrol Number Nine", 11.

107 Ibid., 13; Roscoe, Roscoe, *Submarine Operations in World War II*, 562.

108 Clark, "USS *Trout* (SS 202), Report of War Patrol Number Nine", 15.

109 Ibid., 2.

110 Ibid., 3.

111 Clark, "USS *Trout* (SS 202), Report of War Patrol Number Ten", 5; *Submarine Operations in World War II*, 562; https://www.history.navy.mil/research/histories/ship-histories/danfs/e/ellet.html [accessed 2/20/2024].

112 Clark, "USS *Trout* (SS 202), Report of War Patrol Number Ten", 7.

113 Ibid., 7 & 8; Roscoe, *Submarine Operations in World War II*, 562.

114 Memo: *U.S.S. Trout (SS-202) – loss of.*, the Commander Submarine Force – Pacific Fleet, 17 April 1944 (accompanies last War Patrol Report).

115 http://www.combinedfleet.com/SakitoM_t.htm; http://www.combinedfleet.com/Aki_t.htm; http://www.combinedfleet.com/asashm_t.htm [accessed 2/12/2024].

116 https://www.usna.edu/Chapel/navyhymn.php [accessed 2/12/2024].

117 Page, R. M., "Monostatic Radar" IEEE Trans. ASE, no. ASE-13, no. 2, Sept 1977.

118 *U. S. Submarine Losses – World War II,* NAVPERS 15,784, 1949 Issue, p.90; https://www.oneternalpatrol.com/uss-trout-202.htm [accessed 2/12/2024].

Milton Keynes UK
Ingram Content Group UK Ltd.
UKHW031900260924
448786UK00001B/130